Berlitz

MUNICH & BAVARIA
POCKET GUIDE

Discover the world's best destinations with the Insight Guides Walking Eye app, available to download for free in the App Store and Google Play.

The container app provides easy access to fantastic free content on events and activities taking place in your current location or chosen destination, with the possibility of booking, as well as the regularly-updated Insight Guides travel blog: Inspire Me. In addition, you can purchase curated, premium destination guides through the app, which feature local highlights, hotel, bar, restaurant and shopping listings, an A to Z of practical information and more. Or purchase and download Insight Guides eBooks straight to your device.

TOP 10 ATTRACTIONS

PINAKOTHEK DER MODERNE
The largest museum of art and design in Europe. See page 56.

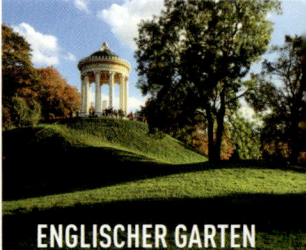

ENGLISCHER GARTEN
Featuring the Chinese Tower and its beer garden. See page 60.

MARIENPLATZ
Munich's main square with the Column of the Virgin Mary at its centre. See page 31.

ALTER PETER
Munich's oldest church provides great views of the city and the Alps. See page 35.

DEUTSCHES MUSEUM
Munich's world class museum of science and technology. See page 64.

ASAMKIRCHE
A theatrical masterpiece of sculpture, decoration and light, created by the Asam brothers. See page 40.

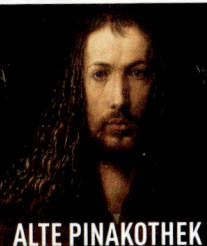

ALTE PINAKOTHEK
One of the world's great art galleries. See page 54.

KÖNIGSSEE
Southern Germany's most attractive and pristine body of water cupped by the High Alps. See page 78.

RESIDENZ
The former royal palace, with seven courtyards and the magnificent Renaissance hall, the Antiquarium. See page 43.

NEUSCHWANSTEIN CASTLE
Ludwig II's extraordinary romanticised version of the medieval world. See page 72.

A PERFECT DAY

9am
Breakfast
A traditional breakfast of sausage with sweet mustard and soft pretzel is the way to start the Munich day; head for Zum Spöckmeier (see page 110) where they guarantee only the freshest Weisswurst.

10am
The Residenz
Kick off your day of Munich sightseeing at the Residenz, slap bang in the city centre. You'll need at least two hours to cover the trio of attractions here – the Residenzmuseum, the Schatzkammer and the Cuvilliés-Theater.

1:30pm
City centre lunch
Take your hunger pangs to Weisses Bräuhaus (see page 110) for some traditional Bavarian fare, or to Prince Myshkin (see page 109) for some lighter, more innovative vegetarian dishes.

12:30pm
Chic shopping
Time to hit the smart boutiques and designer shops at Maximilianstrasse for some retail therapy. Window shop along Residenzstrasse and Theatinerstrasse, by which time you will have worked up a hearty appetite.

2:30pm
Modern art
After lunch, walk to the Museum Quarter for a hefty dose of culture. You'll only have time to view a couple of the multiple venues here, so choose carefully beforehand. Fans of contemporary art and design should head for the multi-coloured Museum Brandhorst and view Andy Warhol's paintings. Refuel in the olde worlde museum café at the nearby Alte Pinakothek.

MUNICH

:30pm

eer gardens

me for a break, so take
short walk from the art
ction to the Englischer
arten for a tranquil
mble and a laze with
e locals on the grass,
erhaps stopping off at
e Chinesischer Turm
see page 112) for a
offee or something
tronger. Afterwards,
eave the park to the
outh to see the river
urfers riding the wave
f the Eisbach stream.

6pm

Mine's a *Stein*

The perfect place to eat and drink your fill is one of
the city's inimitable beer halls. For the full-on tourist
experience you could plump for the Hofbräuhaus (see
page 108); for something a bit more authentic try the
Augustiner Bräustuben (see page 110) located near
Hackerbrücke S-Bahn station or three stops from the
Hauptbahnhof on trams 18 and 19.

8:30pm

All that jazz

A great way to round off the day is an evening at
one of the city's excellent jazz joints. Unterfahrt
im Einstein and Mister B's (see page 90) are the
foot tapping venues of choice. If jazz is not to your
taste, then a more eclectic night scene can be found
near the Ostbahnhof in the shape of Kultfabrik and
Optimolwerke (see page 90) and in the bars of the
Gärtnerplatzviertel.

CONTENTS

- **INTRODUCTION** 10
- **A BRIEF HISTORY** 14
- **WHERE TO GO** 31

In and around Marienplatz 31
Two town halls 32, Frauenkirche 33, Alter Peter 35,
Viktualienmarkt 36, Alter Hof and the Hofbräuhaus 37

To the city gates 38
Eastwards to Isartor 38, Münchner Stadtmuseum 39,
Jüdisches Zentrum 40, Asamkirche 40, Fussgängerzone 41,
Karlsplatz and environs 42

The Residenz and surroundings 43
Residenzmuseum and Treasury 44, The courtyards and
Cuvilliés-Theater 46, Odeonsplatz 47, Ludwigstrasse 49

The Museum Quarter 49
Königsplatz 49, Lenbachhaus 53, Kunstareal München 54

Schwabing 58
Leopoldstrasse 59, Englischer Garten 60, Prinzregentenstrasse 62

Along the Isar 63
Deutsches Museum 64

Outside the city centre 66
Schloss Nymphenburg 66, Olympiapark 69

Into Bavaria 70
Neuschwanstein 71, Oberammergau and Linderhof 73, The
lakes 74, Berchtesgaden 76, North of Munich 78, The Romantic
Road 80, Augsburg 84, Regensburg and around 84, Nuremberg 86

WHAT TO DO 89

- Concerts and opera 89
- Festivals 91
- Shopping 92
- Sports 94
- Children's Munich 96

EATING OUT 99

A–Z TRAVEL TIPS 114

RECOMMENDED HOTELS 132

DICTIONARY 140

INDEX 164

FEATURES

Her name was Lola 22
Beer, bluff and bullets 27
Historical landmarks 29
Karl Valentin 39
Leo von Klenze 51
Schwabing's heyday 59
Degenerate art 60
The Bavarian Alps 75
Nightlife 90
A day at the zoo 97
Calendar of events 98
Seasonal drinking 104

INTRODUCTION

With its relaxed, almost Mediterranean ambience, Munich, the capital of Bavaria, is one of Europe's most engaging cities, one packed with fascinating history, world-class culture and traditional food, and with the outdoor playground of the Alps just a short hop away.

The city's genius has always been its ability to combine the Germanic talent for getting things done with a specifically Bavarian need to do them in an agreeable way. Business lunches always seem a little longer here, and office hours a little shorter. Yet no one who has witnessed the city's impressive affluence, its dynamic car industry and its super-efficient public transport system would suggest that this refreshingly relaxed attitude was unproductive.

Munich and Bavaria are Germany's most popular tourist destinations. According to opinion polls, it's also the city that Germans would most like to call home. It is not just the elegance and prosperity of the place that make it such a magnet, but the lively way of life which is best savoured in one of its many beer gardens, beer halls or just out and about on the town, particularly during the long and usually very hot summers. As the capital of the Catholic and conservative Free State of Bavaria, Munich epitomises the independent Bavarian spirit, but it is also a highly cosmopolitan city, where people from all over the world can and do feel at home.

Of course Munich also plays host to the Oktoberfest, usually the single event that most think of when anyone mentions the city's name. Indeed, with annual consumption of 6.9 million litres of beer by 6.4 million visitors, it is a blockbuster event, quite appropriate to the oversized image the Bavarians have of their capital. It is also the most extravagant expression of that untranslatable feeling of warm fellowship known in German as *Gemütlichkeit*.

CULTURAL CENTRE

But it would be wrong to think of life in Munich merely as one long Oktoberfest. As a result of the post-war division of Berlin, Munich became the undisputed cultural capital of the Federal Republic of Germany – no mean achievement in the face of competition from Hamburg and Cologne. The opera house and concert halls make the town a musical mecca still, especially for performances of works by Richard Strauss, Mozart and Wagner. Wagner's patron was 'mad' King Ludwig II of Bavaria, who was responsible for the fairy-tale Neuschwanstein Castle in the Alpine foothills, but it was his grandfather, Ludwig I, who established the city's cultural credentials by assembling vast collections and building huge edifices in which to store them. That legacy lives on in Munich, and the city is endowed with some world-famous art collections, from the Old Masters of the Alte Pinakothek to the main avantgarde movements represented in the Pinakothek der Moderne and Museum Brandhorst. Painters have long appreciated the favourable artistic climate of the city, particularly in the bohemian district of Schwabing, which exploded onto the international scene in the early 20th century as a centre for the Blaue

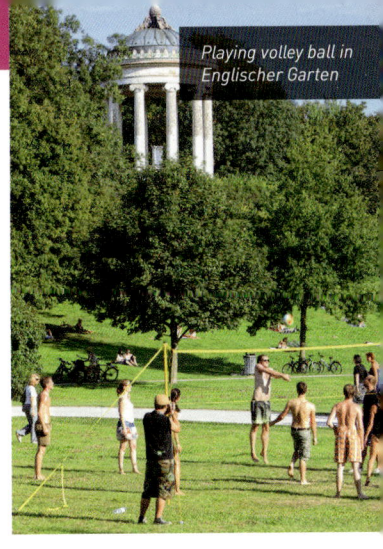

Playing volley ball in Englischer Garten

INTRODUCTION

Vital statistics

Munich is the capital of Bavaria and of the administrative district of Upper Bavaria. It lies on a plain to the north of the Alpine foothills, about 530m (1,700ft) above sea level. The population of the city, which covers about 310 sq km (120 sq miles), is around 1.45 million, making the Bavarian metropolis the third-largest city in Germany, trailing only Berlin and Hamburg.

Reiter school, whose ranks included Wassily Kandinsky, Paul Klee and Franz Marc.

Munich has become a centre for industry and publishing, and also for the much-admired New German Cinema and its world-famous directors, Volker Schloendorff, Werner Herzog and Edgar Reitz. But there is also a darker side to the city, including Adolf Hitler's early association with Munich and the formation here of the Nazi Party. The stormy years from 1918 to 1945 were, in the end, a brief political interlude for the city, and its people seem happy to have relinquished the political limelight to Bonn and Berlin.

RESTORED HERITAGE

Munich has tried, however, to retain its historical identity. After the destruction of World War II, many German cities decided to break with the past and rebuild in a completely modern style. But the authorities in the Bavarian capital chose to painstakingly restore and reconstruct the great churches and palaces of its past. There are plenty of modern office buildings on the periphery, but the heart of the old city has successfully recaptured its rich architectural heritage and charm. There are still some reminders of the ravages of war, and monuments such as the Siegestor (Victory Gate, in Ludwigstrasse) have been left in their bomb-scarred condition as a reminder of more troubled days.

The inner city is a pedestrian's delight, thanks to a clever road system that keeps the majority of the traffic circling the city centre rather than crossing through it (except by means of underpasses) and to an excellent public transport system. Beyond the city centre the broad, tree-lined avenues and boulevards planned by Bavaria's last kings open up the town and provide a considerable touch of elegance.

OPEN SPACES

The Englischer Garten, hemmed by the River Isar, is a real jewel among Europe's great parks. The river's swiftly flowing waters are evidence of the proximity of the Alps, where the river has its source. On a clear day, the Alps seem to lie just south of the city.

When the mountains appear on the city's doorstep, locals are reminded of the countryside from which many of them, or their parents, originated. Every weekend a mass exodus to the surrounding villages and lakes takes place. In the winter many head farther south into the mountains for skiing, an integral part of Bavarian life

Although Munich is undoubtedly a metropolis, the city also retains a resolutely rural atmosphere, never losing sight of its origins in the Bavarian hinterland.

Revellers in the big beer tent at Oktoberfest

A BRIEF HISTORY

Munich was a relatively late arrival on the Bavarian scene. During the Middle Ages, at a time when Nuremberg, Augsburg, Landshut and Regensburg were already thriving cities, the present-day state capital was no more than a small settlement housing some Benedictine monks from Tegernsee. The site was known in the 8th century quite simply as *Ze den Munichen*, a dialect form of *zu den Mönchen* ('the monks' place'). Accordingly, Munich's coat of arms today bears the image of a child in a monk's habit, the Münchner Kindl.

In 1158, the settlement on the River Isar attracted the attention of Heinrich der Löwe (Henry the Lion), the Duke of Saxony and Bavaria, who was cousin of the German Emperor Frederick Barbarossa. He was looking for a place to set up a toll station for the passage of salt, a lucrative product from nearby Salzburg. Until then, tolls had been collected by the powerful bishop of Freising at Oberföhring Bridge, just to the north. Duke Heinrich burned this bridge down and built a new one, together with a market, customs house and mint.

Bishop Otto of Freising was an uncle of Frederick Barbarossa, and protested to the emperor, who decided to leave Munich in Heinrich's hands, but to grant one-third of the toll revenues to the diocese of Freising– dues that were paid until 1852. The day of the emperor's decision, 14 June 1158, is recognised as the date of Munich's foundation.

The salt trade allowed Munich to grow into a prosperous town. In 1180, after Heinrich refused military aid for the emperor's foreign wars, Frederick Barbarossa threatened to raze Munich to the ground. However, Bishop Otto pleaded the city's case, as he was making a great deal of money from his share of the salt duty.

Munich was saved, but the city was handed over to the Wittelsbach family, who ruled Bavaria for the next seven centuries.

THE WITTELSBACHS TAKE OVER

By the end of the 13th century, Munich was the largest town in the Wittelsbach dominions. However, the prosperous Munich burghers grew discontented and began to press Duke Ludwig the Stern (1229–94) for a larger piece of the pie. In defence, the duke built himself a fortress, the Alter Hof, parts of which still stand near Marienplatz.

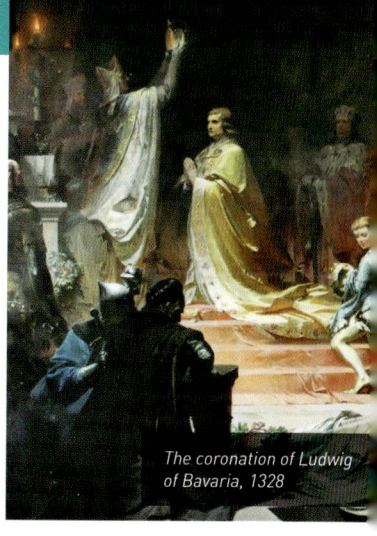
The coronation of Ludwig of Bavaria, 1328

Munich entered the international political arena in 1328, when Duke Ludwig IV (1294–1347) was made Holy Roman Emperor. With his court firmly established in Munich, he enlisted scholars from all over Europe as his advisors. Perhaps the most notable of these were Marsiglio of Padua and the English Franciscan friar William of Occam, both philosophers who defended secular power against that of the Pope and thus made themselves useful allies for Ludwig.

TROUBLED TIMES

The Black Death brought devastation in 1348. The city suffered social unrest and abrupt economic decline. In an irrational reaction to the catastrophe, citizens went on a wild rampage, massacring Jews for alleged ritual murder.

High taxes caused the burghers to revolt against the patricians. In 1385, the people beheaded a cloth merchant, Hans Impler, on the Schrannenplatz (now Marienplatz), the patricians and their princes demanded financial compensation, and the situation deteriorated into open rebellion from 1397 to 1403.

By bringing in heavy military reinforcements, the Wittelsbachs regained the upper hand without being forced to make the far-reaching civic concessions won by the guilds in other German cities. To secure their position during these troubled times, the Wittelsbachs built a sturdy fortress, the Residenz, on what was then the northern edge of town.

REFORM AND COUNTER-REFORM

Dissent eased in the 15th century, and trade boomed in salt, wine and cloth and the town also served as a transit point for spices and gold. The great Frauenkirche and the Gothic civic citadel of the Altes Rathaus, were built during this period of renewed prosperity.

By the mid-16th century, an architectural rivalry had grown up between the burghers, who favoured the German Gothic style for their homes, and the Bavarian nobles, who preferred the Renaissance styles of southern Europe. The appearance of Munich in the 1500s is preserved in Jakob Sandtner's city model on display in the Bavarian National Museum. However, most of the original buildings were later replaced by the baroque and rococo palaces of the 17th and 18th centuries and

Simplest is best

Regarded as one of the major figures of medieval thought, William of Occam is best known for 'Occam's Razor', in which he states, roughly, that if you've found a simple explanation for a problem, don't look for a complicated one. Bavarians like that kind of thinking.

the neo-Gothic and neo-classical buildings of the Industrial Revolution.

The Bavarian aristocracy's preference for foreign styles was in many ways a reaction to the subversive implications of German nationalism, which had grown out of the Reformation. In 1510, when Martin Luther passed through Munich on his way to Rome, his still relatively orthodox preaching met with sympathy. But some 10 years later Luther's revolutionary position aroused the anger of the traditionally conservative Bavarians, and Duke Wilhelm IV introduced the severe measures advocated by the Jesuits. Rebellious monks and priests were arrested and executed.

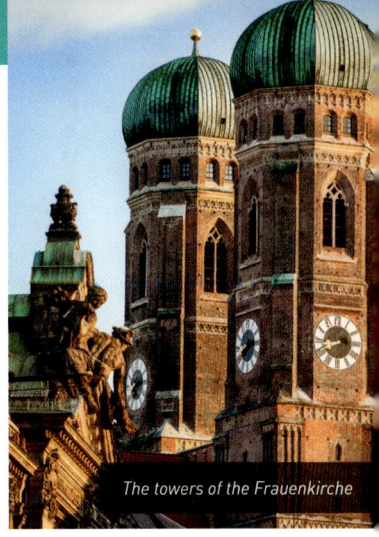

The towers of the Frauenkirche

The religious conflict concealed a competition for political and economic power. The city's bourgeoisie had seen in the Reformation an opportunity to push for the social reforms which the aristocracy had adamantly resisted. In the struggles that followed, the burghers were forced to relinquish the salt monopoly to the administration of the state.

With a certain vindictiveness, the nobles flaunted their political triumph with sumptuous festivities at court, such as those arranged to pay homage to Emperor Charles V and his Spanish retinue during their visit in 1530. The climax of such pomp and circumstance was the three-week-long wedding celebration of Duke Wilhelm V and his bride, Renata of Lorraine, in 1568.

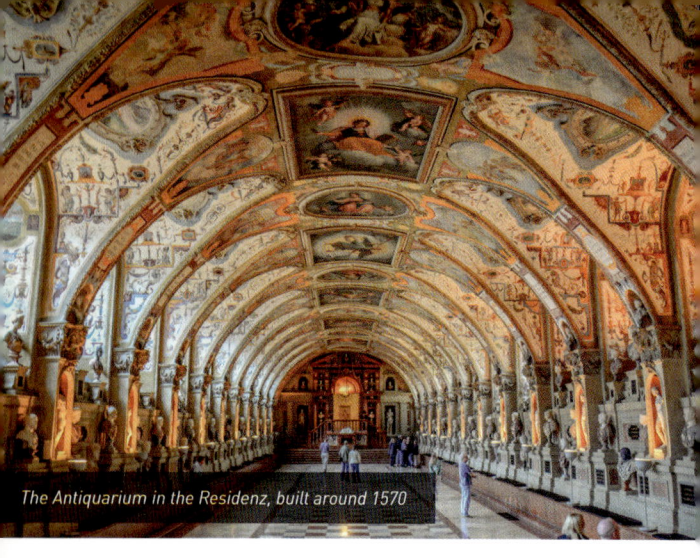

The Antiquarium in the Residenz, built around 1570

GOOD MONEY AFTER BAD

Such extravagant expenditure meant that the state coffers were empty by the time Maximilian I (1573–1651) came to the throne. Despite this lack of funds, Maximilian (who was made Prince Elector in 1623) proceeded to build up a magnificent collection of art works. However painful this may have been for his tax-crippled subjects, we can be thankful to him for having thus laid the foundations of the Alte Pinakothek.

It was also Maximilian who ordered the splendid decorations that embellish the Residenz. Gustavus Adolphus of Sweden, who invaded Munich in 1632 during the cruel Thirty Years' War, was so impressed with the Residenz that he expressed a wish to wheel the whole thing back to Stockholm. Instead, he settled for 42 Munich citizens, who were taken hostage against payment by Bavaria of 300,000 Thaler in war reparations. All but six of them returned three years later.

The Thirty Years' War (1618–48), caused less damage in Munich than in many other German towns. However, starvation and disease wrought more havoc than the cannon. In 1634 the Black Death struck, killing 7,000 inhabitants – a third of the city's population. In 1638, Maximilian set up the Mariensäule (Column of the Virgin Mary) as thanks for the city's deliverance.

Munich's Prince Electors frequently involved the city in costly foreign adventures, thus rubbing salt into the wounds of civic poverty. In 1683, Maximilian II Emanuel decided to help the Austrians beat off the Turks besieging Vienna. He promptly set out for Belgrade, and returned bringing 296 Turks as sedan-chair bearers and road-builders. The Turkish Wars are commemorated in huge paintings that are on display in Schleissheim Castle. The city was saddled with an immense debt as a result of the war.

During the War of the Spanish Succession (1701–14) Maximilian II Emanuel fought, along with the French, on the losing side and Munich had to bear the unfortunate burden of Austrian occupation from 1704 to 1714. When the farmers rebelled in 1705, the ringleaders were arrested and hanged, drawn and quartered on Marienplatz.

After the war, the Bavarian aristocracy was not especially sympathetic to the tribulations of the citizenry. They began building palaces for themselves, including the Preysing Palais, the Archbishop's Palais and the Törring-Jettenbach Palais.

PEACE IN AN ENGLISH GARDEN

The people of Munich grew ever more xenophobic after Hungarian hussars took over the city in 1742. They were dispatched by Empress Maria Theresa in retaliation for the Bavarian Prince Elector's opposition to Austro-Hungarian involvement in Germany.

HISTORY

In this atmosphere of hostility, Maximilian III Joseph (1727–77) could not have been surprised when the Munich bourgeoisie resisted his efforts to establish a court monopoly on the manufacture of goods. All the royal manufacturers went bankrupt, with the exception of Nymphenburg porcelain (still a thriving concern). A brighter note was struck with the building of the delightful Cuvilliés-Theater and the performance there by one Wolfgang Amadeus Mozart of his operas *Idomeneo* (premiered there in 1781), *The Abduction from the Seraglio*, *The Marriage of Figaro* and *The Magic Flute*.

When Maximilian III Joseph, the last of the true Wittelsbach line, died in 1777, the succession fell to Karl Theodor, a member of the Mannheim branch of the family. He didn't want to leave Mannheim, he didn't like Munich and Munich didn't like him. The people were starving. Instead of bread, Karl Theodor sent in soldiers to suppress the angry populace.

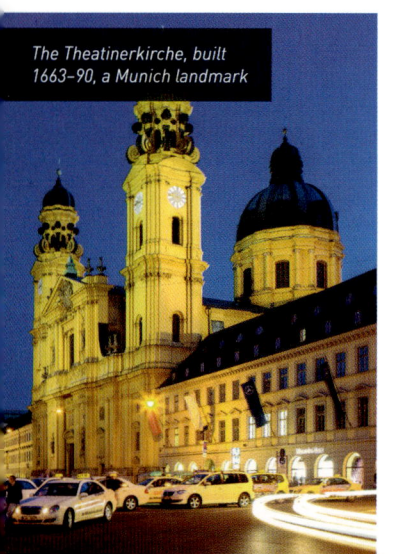
The Theatinerkirche, built 1663–90, a Munich landmark

It was Benjamin Thompson, an American, who suggested a solution to Karl Theodor's predicament. With the prince's blessing, Count Rumford (as he was subsequently known) provided schools and work to keep the unruly soldiers off the streets. He set up workshops and soup kitchens for the poor. In 1789, Rumford requisitioned a marshy wilderness on the outskirts of town and detailed the soldiers to drain it for development as gardens and a gigantic public park – today's Englischer Garten.

HOPES AND DREAMS

While Munich was gardening, Europe was in revolutionary uproar and the city could not remain immune to these events for long. In 1800 it was occupied by the French troops of General Jean Victor Moreau, who established his headquarters in Nymphenburg Palace.

Napoleon himself arrived in 1805 for the wedding of his wife Josephine's son, Eugène de Beauharnais, to Princess Augusta. The emperor was on his way to Austerlitz (in today's Czech Republic), where he was to fight the Russians and Austrians. Napoleon elevated Maximilian IV Joseph from Prince Elector to King of Bavaria, and in exchange took a vast contingent of Bavarians on his Russian campaign of 1812. Under pressure from the French, Maximilian emancipated the Protestants of Munich, improved conditions for the Jews and introduced a more moderate constitution.

Despite the troubles of war and revolution, Munich managed to celebrate once again. Heeding the new spirit of the times, the royal court chose not to exclude the populace from the celebrations in honour of the marriage of Maximilian's son, Ludwig, to Theresa of Saxony. On 17 October 1810, horseraces were organised, with great success. These morphed into an annual event which became known as Oktoberfest.

Munich itself was gradually expanding to the north and west into Maxvorstadt, a region that links the city centre to Schwabing. The Graeco-Roman architecture of the Nationaltheater brought to the city the first signs of the Classical spirit that was to become the obsession of Ludwig I.

Born in Strasbourg, Ludwig (1786–1868) was determined to break the French stranglehold on German culture and to make Munich the leader of a new nationalist movement. During the Napoleonic occupation, the civic symbol of the Münchner Kindl had been replaced with an imperial lion; Ludwig made sure that the little monk was restored.

Familiar with the architecture of Greece and Rome, Ludwig wanted to turn Munich into an 'Athens-on-the-Isar'. His first step was to move Bavaria's university from Landshut to Munich, where it was established along Ludwigstrasse.

Königsplatz, with its Greek Revival architecture, was the most complete realisation of Ludwig's Classical aspirations. Typically, Ludwig himself laid the foundation stone for the Alte Pinakothek (the gallery designed to house the royal art collections) on 7

⊙ HER NAME WAS LOLA

A prodigious worker, rising before dawn each day to go to his office in the Residenz, Ludwig I gained some diversion from his sober duties by commissioning a series of portraits of the most beautiful young women of Munich. The collection hangs in the Schönheitsgalerie (Gallery of Beautiful Women) at the Nymphenburg Palace. Included is his mistress, a dancer known as Lola Montez, with whom he fell in love when he was 60 and she 28. She was Ludwig's ruin. He made her the Countess von Landsfeld, to the horror both of his conservative ministers and the radical university students.

In 1848, as revolution swept Europe, the students and angry citizens of Munich forced Ludwig to deport Lola, and he abdicated in disgust. The story of Lola's fascinatingly eventful life is told in the book *Lola Montez: A Life* by Bruce Seymour.

April 1826, the anniversary of the painter Raphael's birth. Ludwig's successor Maximilian II (1811– 64) boosted Munich's cultural reputation thanks to his intimacy with illustrious thinkers such as the historian Leopold von Ranke, the philosopher Friedrich von Schelling and the chemist Justus von Liebig.

Ludwig II

END OF A DREAM

The last great king of Bavaria was the romantic king Ludwig II (1845–86), famous for his collaboration with Richard Wagner. Under Ludwig's patronage, the composer staged in Munich the premières of his operas *Tristan und Isolde*, *Die Meistersinger von Nürnberg*, *Das Rheingold* and *Die Walküre*.

In the mundane world of 19th-century industrial expansion, Ludwig dreamt of making Munich the music capital of the world. He wanted to build a gigantic theatre for his idol Wagner, a place where the composer could develop his concept of *Gesamtkunstwerk* – a synthesis of music, lyrics and theatre. State finances forced him to relinquish the project to Bayreuth.

Ludwig acted out his fantasies in the eccentric palaces he built outside Munich – a medieval castle at Neuschwanstein, a beautiful French château at Linderhof and a fanciful version of Versailles' Grand Trianon at Herrenchiemsee (more were planned). Ironically, it was at the 16th-century castle, Schloss Berg by Lake Starnberg, that Ludwig's life came to a mysterious

HISTORY

end. By 1886, his unorthodox behaviour had persuaded the Bavarian government that he was insane, and a special commission 'confirmed' this. The director of a mental asylum accompanied him to Schloss Berg but the two were later found drowned. Was it murder or suicide? The speculation continues to this day.

Uncle Luitpold took over as regent (in place of Ludwig's brother, the insane King Otto). He presided over the grand fin de siècle artistic movement of the *Jugendstil*. This was followed a generation later by the *Blaue Reiter* (Blue Rider) school, which included Wassily Kandinsky, Paul Klee, Franz Marc and Gabriele Münter. Thomas Mann, Rainer Maria Rilke, Stefan George and other writers moved to Schwabing. The artistic ferment also attracted a painter from Vienna, a young man named Adolf Hitler.

The Wittelsbach dynasty, along with others in Vienna and Berlin, ended in the disaster of World War I. Bavarians resented having been dragged into the European conflict by what they felt was Prussian belligerence, and a new social democratic movement gained support. In November 1918, Kurt Eisner led a march of workers and peasants from the Theresienwiese. En route, disaffected soldiers took control of their barracks and hoisted the red flag of revolution. The Bavarian Socialist Republic was declared in the Mathäser Bräuhaus. The people invaded the Residenz and Ludwig III, the last Wittelsbach king, fled in a car from the palace.

But the newly born republic of workers, peasants and soldiers, modelled on the Soviets created under the Russian revolution, was subject to violent attack from the conservative press and from private armies of troops *(Freikorps)*. Playing on Bavarian xenophobia, the right wing attacked Eisner as a Berliner and as a Jew. Just three months after the November revolution, Eisner was dead, shot down by a young aristocrat hoping to curry favour with an extreme right-wing club.

'Der Blaue Reiter' by Wassily Kandinsky

A group of 'coffee-house anarchists' led by the writers Ernst Toller and Erich Mühsam took over briefly, but they were soon replaced by hard-line communists. After fierce and bloody fighting with the Freikorps, the Bavarian Red Army was defeated, and the short-lived independent republic of Bavaria was crushed.

HITLER'S MUNICH

Adolf Hitler had first been drawn to Munich by its cultural ambience, but he remained immune to the innovative tendencies of the avant-garde. His own painting was stolidly academic and attracted no attention. He turned to the clamour of German nationalism, and a chance photograph taken at a rally on Odeonsplatz in August 1914 shows Hitler in the crowd, joyfully greeting news of the declaration of war.

He returned to Munich as a corporal in 1918. It was while working to re-educate soldiers in nationalistic, anti-Marxist

Marching for the Bavarian Republic in 1919

ideas at the end of the Bavarian Republic that he joined the Deutsche Arbeiter-Partei. By February 1920, he was able to address 2,000 members in the Hofbräuhaus. The association soon became known as the Nationalsozialistische Deutsche Arbeiter-Partei, or Nazi Party. Its symbol was the swastika. Armed storm troops of the party's Sturm-Abteilung (SA) broke up any opposition political meetings held in Munich.

At a January 1923 meeting, Hitler declared: 'Either the Nazi Party is the German movement of the future, in which case no devil can stop it, or it isn't, in which case it deserves to be destroyed'. Both proved true. By November, the party had 55,000 members and 15,000 storm troops. Hitler then felt strong enough to stage his famous Beer Hall Putsch.

This was intended as a first move in the campaign to force the Bavarian state government to cooperate in a Nazi march on Berlin. The putsch ended in a debacle on Odeonsplatz with

HITLER'S MUNICH

Hitler being sent to prison, but not before he had turned the whole affair to his advantage. He ensured that his trial for treason became an indictment of his prosecutors as accomplices of the 'November criminals' who, he said, had stabbed Germany in the back in 1918 with their anti-war movement. Hitler became an instant hero. In prison at nearby Landsberg, he was not required to perform prison duties, but instead held political meetings and used his time to write his manifesto, *Mein Kampf*.

Hitler's career took him to Berlin, but the Nazis kept their party headquarters in Munich at the Brown House (named after the colour of their shirts). Brighter spirits of the time, including the whimsical comedian Karl Valentin and a fan of his, the dramatist Bertolt Brecht, also made their home in Munich.

In 1935, Munich became known as the 'Capital of the (Nazi) Movement'. Its status at the vanguard was confirmed in June

⊙ BEER, BLUFF AND BULLETS

The Beer Hall Putsch, which launched Hitler's national career, was staged in the now defunct Bürgerbräukeller. It gave a foretaste of the crazy melodrama, bluff and shameless gall he was later to exhibit on the world scene.

With the Bavarian minister Gustav von Kahr about to speak, Hitler burst into the crowded room, smashed a beer mug to the floor, and pushed forward at the head of his storm troops, brandishing a pistol. In the pandemonium, he jumped on a table and fired a shot into the ceiling. 'National revolution has broken out!' he yelled. 'Farce! South America!' was the response from a few wags, who were promptly beaten up. The new Hitler style of politics had indisputably arrived. Today Hilton City Hotel stands on the site and there is no plaque commemorating the putsch.

1938, when the central synagogue was looted, presaging the *Kristallnacht* (Night of Broken Glass) rampage five months later, when Jewish premises across Germany were attacked.

In September of that year, Munich also became a symbol of the ignominious appeasement decisions by Britain and France. In Munich's Führerbau, a meeting took place between prime ministers Neville Chamberlain and Edouard Daladier, during which they negotiated the dismemberment of Czechoslovakia with Hitler and Mussolini. Later, Chamberlain obtained a signed piece of paper from the Führer, a guarantee he claimed of 'peace in our time'.

WAR AND PEACE

Large-scale resistance to the Nazis was not possible in wartime Munich, but there were voices of dissent including the *Weisse Rose* student movement, which distributed anti-Hitler leaflets at the university. But the founders, Hans and Sophie Scholl and Christoph Probst, were guillotined on 22 February 1943.

A total of 71 air raids hit the city during World War II, killing 6,000 and wounding 16,000. Attacks were most intense in 1944, heavily damaging the Frauenkirche, St Peter's and St Michael's churches, and parts of the Residenz and Alte Pinakothek. The city still remembers the dark days of the Third Reich and is not afraid to talk about it.

Post-war reconstruction was a triumph of hard work and loyal attachment to the great traditions of Munich's past. Monuments, palaces and churches were restored with care. Open to the arts and good living, Munich expanded and became Germany's third-largest city, welcoming Berliners and refugees.

The city continues to build on its international reputation as a city of culture, with a year-round programme of performing arts productions. Visitors to Munich can be sure of a taste of good living, Bavarian-style.

HISTORICAL LANDMARKS

8th century Small settlement of Benedictine monks gives the site its name.
1158 Henry the Lion sets up toll station for the salt trade from Salzburg.
1180 Emperor Frederick Barbarossa takes Munich from Henry and hands the city over to the Wittelsbach family.
1328 Duke Ludwig IV becomes Holy Roman Emperor and his court is established in Munich.
1348 Black Death brings devastation to Munich.
15th century A period of prosperity – Transit point for trade from Venice.
1632 Swedish armies invade Munich during the Thirty Years' War.
1638 Mariensäule erected on Marienplatz.
1704–1714 Austrian occupation of Munich.
1742 Hungarian hussars take over the city.
1789 American Benjamin Thompson develops the Englischer Garten.
1805 Napoleon visits Munich.
1806 Napoleon raises Bavaria to status of kingdom.
1826 Ludwig I lays the foundation stone for the Alte Pinakothek.
1845 Bavarian King Ludwig II is born.
1886 Ludwig II found drowned in Lake Starnberg close to Schloss Berg.
1918 The Bavarian Republic declared. Ludwig III flees.
1919 Kurt Eisner, leader of a short-lived socialist regime, assassinated.
1923 Adolf Hitler stages his famous 'Beer Hall Putsch'.
1935 Munich named capital of the Nazi Movement.
1939–1945 World War II: 71 air raids on the city, killing 6,000.
1972 Munich hosts the Summer Olympic Games.
2002 Pinakothek der Moderne opened. Germany adopts the euro.
2006 Jewish Museum of Munich opened at St-Jakobs-Platz.
2009 Museum Brandhorst opened.
2012 Munich celebrates 200 years of the beer garden. Artworks stolen during the Nazi period are rediscovered.
2015 NS-Dokumentationszentrum opened.
2017 Angela Merkel wins a fourth term as Chancellor in federal elections, but no party receives an outright majority in any state, including Bavaria.

The Neue Rathaus in Marienplatz

WHERE TO GO

Munich has two enormous assets as far as the visitor is concerned. First, a large majority of the city's museums, monuments, palaces and churches are concentrated in the Innenstadt (inner city), which makes Munich a great place to explore on foot. Second, Munich's public transport, incorporating buses, trams, underground (U-Bahn) and suburban trains (S-Bahn), brings all the other sights within easy reach so there is no need for a car.

Munich long ago expanded beyond the confines of its medieval boundaries, and the old city wall long since disappeared. However, the remains of three gates survive marking out the perimeter of the inner city – Isartor, Karlstor and Sendlinger Tor – as well as Odeonsplatz, a rendezvous for salt traders setting off in the 14th century for northern Germany. Ever since Munich's earliest beginnings, however, Marienplatz has been at the heart of it all.

IN AND AROUND MARIENPLATZ

Until the middle of the 19th century, **Marienplatz** ❶ was the place where the wheat market was held. The square was the obvious site for the town hall, and was the place where criminals were hanged. Marienplatz was also the scene of the most extravagant wedding Munich has ever seen – that of Duke Wilhelm V to Renata of Lorraine in 1568. It was the inevitable choice for the central interchange of the U-Bahn and S-Bahn system in 1972.

Marienplatz today forms part of an attractive pedestrian zone and is home of the **Mariensäule** (Column of the Virgin Mary),

IN AND AROUND MARIENPLATZ

erected in 1638 by Maximilian I in gratitude for the town's deliverance from the Plague after its defeat by the Swedes during the Thirty Years' War. At the base of the column are a basilisk, dragon, serpent and lion – which represent plague, hunger, heresy and war – each being vanquished by heroic cherubs. On the top of the monument is the gilded figure of Mary, who watches over Munich. Holding Jesus in her left arm and a sceptre in her right, she is a reminder of Munich's religious foundation. The square also contains the 19th-century **Fischbrunnen** monument. Young butchers used to leap into the bronze fountain at the end of their apprenticeship, but today the tradition is kept up only by Fasching (carnival) revellers or raucous soccer fans.

TWO TOWN HALLS

Standing at the eastern end of Marienplatz is the picturesque **Altes Rathaus** ❷ (Old Town Hall), an example of Munich's efforts to rebuild, rather than replace, the remnants of its venerable history. The dove-grey facade, amber-tiled steeple and graceful little spires of this Gothic-style edifice capture the spirit of the 15th-century original designed by Jörg von Halsbach (alias Jörg Ganghofer), though it isn't an exact replica. In any case, with the addition over the centuries of a baroque, onion-shaped cupola and then an overzealous 'regothification', the building that was destroyed by Allied bombs was probably further from the original than what you see today. Adjacent to the main building, the clock tower provides the perfect setting for the **Spielzeugmuseum** (Toy Museum; daily 10am–5.30pm; charge). Fascinating collections, ranging from antique train sets to animals in the zoo, are spread over four floors linked by a spiral staircase.

The Old Town Hall contains a banqueting hall, but the daily business of city government takes place at the **Neues**

Rathaus (New Town Hall) on the northern side of the square. This is a fine example of 19th-century Neo-Gothic architecture, proud and self-assertive with a facade elaborately decorated with the statues of kings, princes and dukes, saints, allegorical figures and characters from Munich folklore. The tower is 85m (260ft) high; its main attraction, apart from the splendid view (lift to the top; May–Oct daily 10am–7pm, Nov–Apr Mon–Fri 10am–5pm) is the 43-bell **Glockenspiel** (carillon) which puts on three shows daily, at 11am, noon (plus 5pm in summer). Two groups of figures appear, one group re-enacting the tournament held during the wedding of Duke Wilhelm V and Renata of Lorraine and the other, underneath, recreating the cooper's dance *(Schäfflertanz)*, which was performed to cheer up the surviving populace after the plague of 1517. In the evening, at 9pm, a night watchman with lantern blows his horn and an angel of peace blesses the little Munich monk (Münchner Kindl).

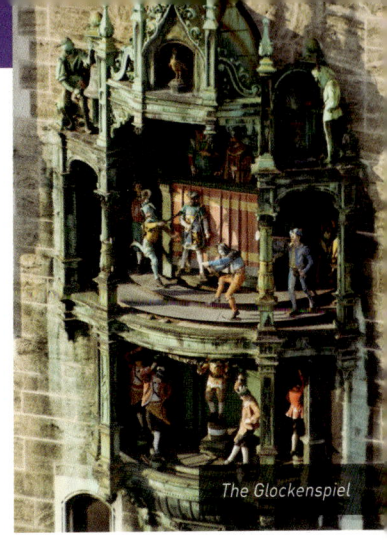

The Glockenspiel

FRAUENKIRCHE

Now head along Weinstrasse (from the west side of Marienplatz) and left along Sporerstrasse to reach Frauenplatz and the enormous Domkirche zu Unserer Lieben Frau (Cathedral Church of Our Lady), usually referred to simply as the **Frauenkirche** ❸ (daily 7am–7pm). With its twin brick towers and their bulbous domes (99m/325ft high) dominating the centre of the city, this church has always been Munich's defining landmark. An austere, unadorned Gothic structure, it was built between 1468 and 1488 by Jörg von Halsbach (aka Jörg Ganghofer). The Italian Renaissance domes are a 1524 addition.

The stark interior was reconstructed from the rubble of World War II bombardments – a truly heroic work of restoration. The original Gothic windows in the choir, stored safely away during the war, give an impression of the church's former glory. Fine sculptures of the Apostles and Prophets also escaped destruction and adorn the choir as before. They were created by Erasmus Grasser in 1502. Dating from 1483 a fine altarpiece by Friedrich Pacher, the *Baptism of Christ*, hangs in the north chapel. It is flanked by Jan Polack's panels depicting Jesus on the Mount of Olives and his arrest, crucifixion and burial. Notice, too, the 17th-century funerary monument of Emperor Ludwig the Bavarian, who died in 1347.

It's possible to ascend the **South Tower** by lift for a unique view of the city (Apr–Oct Mon–Sat 10am–5pm; charge).

> **Devil's footprint**
>
> In addition to its twin towers, the Frauenkirche is known for its 'Devil's Footprint'. Jörg von Halsbach made a pact with the devil that in return for the money to complete the church he would design it without any visible windows. This was but an illusion, however, there being just one point near the entrance from which no windows could be seen. Thus deceived, the devil stamped his foot in fury; both imprint and illusion can be seen to this day.

ALTER PETER

Looming over the south side of Marienplatz, but not quite on the square itself, is **St Peter's** ❹, Munich's oldest church, dating from before the foundation of the city itself in 1158, hence it's nickname Alter Peter – Old Peter. The original structure gave way to a building in the Romanesque style, succeeded in time by a Gothic church that boasted a twin-steepled tower. Everything but the tower was obliterated in the great fire of 1327, and a new Gothic structure went up. This was remodelled along Renaissance lines in the 17th century, and a new tower with a single steeple was created. Destroyed in the war, St Peter's has been faithfully reconstructed. It's well worth climbing the 306 steps to the observation balcony at the top for the stunning views over the city (entrance off Rindermarkt; Mon–Fri 9am–6.30pm, Sat and Sun 10am–6.30pm, winter until 5.30pm).

The tower of the Alter Peter

The crowning piece of the light, bright interior is the **high altar** glorifying Peter and the fathers of the Church. It was restored from the remnants of the 18th-century original, inspired by Bernini's altar for St Peter's in Rome. Egid Quirin Asam (see page 40) was the designer of the ensemble, incorporating Erasmus Grasser's *St Peter*. The gilded wood figures of the Church fathers are the masterly work of Egid Quirin. Leading up to the altar are splendid rococo choir stalls. You'll also see five of Jan Polack's

Inside the Alter Hof

Late Gothic paintings that once adorned the altar. They show Peter healing the lame, enthroned, at sea, in prison and on the cross. Also from the Late Gothic period is the Schrenk Altar, a fine early 15th-century sandstone relief of the Crucifixion and the Day of Judgment.

VIKTUALIENMARKT

Just behind St Peter's, at the other side of Rosenstrasse, lies one of the most colourful locations in Munich and a magnet for all who love food, the **Viktualienmarkt** ❺. The city's central market has been trading here since 1807. Stroll around the enticing stalls with their myriad cheeses and exotic spices, breads, meats, fruit and vegetables. The cheerful atmosphere of the market makes it the perfect place for annual performances of the Marketwomen's Dance, held on Shrove Tuesday. It's also the scene of a number of lively celebrations around the flower-bedecked maypole.

Adjacent to the Viktualienmarkt is **Heiliggeistkirche** (Church of the Holy Spirit). This 14th-century Gothic structure was extensively altered to suit the baroque tastes of the 1720s. The two styles come together perfectly in the **Marienaltar** – a lovely wooden sculpture of 1450, the *Hammerthaler Muttergottes* (Hammerthal Mother of God) originally from the Lake Tegernsee monastery, set in a gilded baroque frame. The high altar preserves a fine pair of *Adoring Angels* from 1730 by Johann Georg Greiff.

ALTER HOF AND THE HOFBRÄUHAUS

Coming out of the church, duck along little Burgstrasse past the Altes Rathaus. Pause at No. 5 to admire the **Hofer** restaurant (see page 109). One of only a handful of Gothic houses still left in Munich, this was once the home of the town clerk. Built in about 1550, it has a neatly restored leafy courtyard and a staircase tower.

Continue along Burgstrasse to the **Alter Hof**, Munich's old royal residence, which was originally built in 1255 by Ludwig the Stern in the then northeastern part of the city. It was designed as a defence against foreign invaders as well as the city's own unruly burghers, but was eventually superseded by the Residenz (see page 43). The buildings suffered more at the hands of 19th-century urban developers than during the 20th-century bombing. However, as you pass through the gates into the courtyard you'll see that parts of the complex have been superbly restored. The reconstructed Burgtor (City Gate) and quaint little Affenturm (Monkey Tower) in the west wing recapture the atmosphere of the Wittelsbachs' first Munich residence as it was in the 15th century. The heraldic painting on the tower came to light during the 1960s.

Turn right on Pfisterstrasse to Platzl (Little Square), the site of a building of no great architectural distinction but one of Munich's greatest attractions, the **Hofbräuhaus** ❻ (Royal Brewery) beer hall. Duke Wilhelm V founded a brewery in the Alter Hof in 1589 to avoid paying the high prices for imported beer from Hanover. Beer has always been just as popular among the aristocracy as with the common people of Bavaria. It replaced wine as the staple alcoholic beverage after the Bavarian vineyards were destroyed by the cruel winters of the 13th and 14th centuries, making way for the sturdier hop and barley crops.

The brewery was first established in the royal bath house, and moved to these more spacious quarters in 1644. The Hofbräuhaus itself was built in 1896, after the brewery was

Playing in the Hofbräuhaus

transferred to the other side of the River Isar. It soon became the most prestigious of Munich's many political beer-hall arenas. In November 1921, Hitler's storm troops first gained notoriety in what became known as the *Schlacht im Hofbräuhaus* (Battle of the Hofbräuhaus). Today, the huge beer hall, with its long tables and oompah music, is a magnet for tourists.

TO THE CITY GATES

Beyond Marienplatz and its immediate surroundings, there are many more sights to discover in Munich's Innenstadt (inner city). They're reached by following the main historic arteries leading from Marienplatz to the old city gates.

EASTWARDS TO ISARTOR

Just south of the Hofbräuhaus is another venerable Munich institution, the **Weisses Bräuhaus**, the beer hall/restaurant of the Schneider Brewery, known for its *Weissbier* (wheat beer). Proceed eastwards along Tal to the **Isartor**, the only city gate that retains its original 14th-century dimensions. Put up in the days when the Bavarian Duke Ludwig IV was Holy Roman Emperor, a later fresco on the gate dating from 1835 shows him returning triumphantly from victory over the Habsburgs.

MÜNCHNER STADTMUSEUM

The walk to Sendlinger Tor takes you past the municipal museum and through the busy shopping area of Sendlinger Strasse. From the southeast corner of Marienplatz, follow Rindermarkt past St Peter's Church. The street soon widens into a square, the centre of which holds the **Rinderbrunnen** (cattle fountain), designed by Joseph Henselmann.

From here cut across Rosental and into St-Jakobs-Platz to visit the unmissable **Münchner Stadtmuseum** ❼ (Munich City Museum; Tue–Sun 10am–6pm; www.muenchner-stadtmuseum.de; charge). Completely remodelled in 2008 to celebrate Munich's 500th birthday, the main Typisch München (Typically Munich) exhibition here takes a comprehensive look at the Bavarian capital's past through a series of themes, periods and personalities. All aspects of the city's story are dealt with, from the Frauenkirche and Schäfflertanz to Lola Montez and Nymphenburg porcelain. A separate annexe houses the Nationalsozialismus in München exhibition, which examines the role of Munich in the rise of the Nazis. Allow at least two hours to see everything.

⊙ KARL VALENTIN

Although little known outside Germany, Karl Valentin was regarded by connoisseurs as a comic genius equal to Charlie Chaplin. While resident in Munich in the early 1920s, the dramatist Bertolt Brecht went almost every night to watch Valentin's portrayal of the clownish, working-class characters of peasant origin who were so peculiar to the city.

Munich's artists and intellectuals loved Valentin's insane, surreal logic. One of his most celebrated sketches portrayed an attempt to house birds in an aquarium and fish in a birdcage.

The Ohel Jakob Synagogue on St-Jakobs-Platz

JÜDISCHES ZENTRUM

In the centre of the square, an austere ensemble of cuboid buildings forms the **Jüdisches Zentrum am Jakobsplatz** ❽ (Jakobsplatz Jewish Centre), consisting of the Ohel Jakob Synagogue, the Jewish Community Centre and the **Jüdisches Museum** (Tue–Sun 10am–6pm; www.juedisches-museum-muenchen.de; charge). Guided tours allow visitors to see the synagogue, while the museum's permanent exhibition 'Voices_Places_Times' shows the history of the Jewish community in and around Munich in a series of installations. A major focus is directed towards Jewish festivals past and present and contemporary aspects of the Jewish religion. The centre offers a wide range of events including concerts and lectures.

ASAMKIRCHE

From the Jewish Museum cross Oberanger and continue up the short Hermann-Sack-Strasse to arrive in Sendlinger Strasse. Amidst the shops on the right-hand side (No. 62) rises the famous Church of St John Nepomuk, better known as the **Asamkirche** ❾ after its creator, the Bavarian architect and sculptor Egid Quirin Asam (1692–1750). This master of late-baroque illusion had wanted to build his own private church here, but was forced to make it accessible to the public after fierce local resistance. The foundation stone was laid in 1733, and the consecration took place in 1746. Asam was assisted in the design by his brother, Cosmas Damian, who specialised in fresco painting. The result is one of the most astonishing achievements of Bavarian baroque. The interior is a theatrical masterpiece of sculpture, decoration and light; the **high altar** leads the eye up to a large Crucifixion dominated by a representation of God the Father wearing the papal crown.

Next door is the **Asamhaus**, where Egid Quirin lived. It was built at the same time as the church, and again with the assistance of Cosmas Damian. It's worth studying the intricate facade. Secure in their Catholic faith, the Asam brothers happily mixed pagan and Christian figures in their decorative schemes. At the end of Sendlinger Strasse, only two hexagonal towers remain from the 14th-century **Sendlinger Tor**.

FUSSGÄNGERZONE

West of Marienplatz, Kaufingerstrasse leads into Neuhauser Strasse, both of them forming the longest section of Munich's **Fussgängerzone** (pedestrian precinct), busy with shoppers and popular with summertime buskers. At the corner of Neuhauser Strasse and Augustinerstrasse is the former Augustinian church; in Napoleonic times it became a customs house and much later, in 1966, a museum of hunting and fishing, the **Deutsches Jagd- und Fischereimuseum** (daily 9.30am–5pm, Thur until 9pm; charge). Fronted by a wild boar in bronze, the collection will fascinate hunters, anglers and children alike.

Further along Neuhauser Strasse is the 16th-century **St Michael's**, an Italian Renaissance church with baroque overtones (the first of its kind in Germany), designed by the Dutch architect Friedrich Sustris. St Michael's epitomises the combative spirit of the Counter-Reformation, and it is fitting that the Wittelsbach

Asamkirche interior

dukes and German emperors, the secular defenders of the faith, are depicted on the gabled facade. Above the entrance, third figure from the right, stands the church's founder, Duke Wilhelm V (with a model of the church in his hand). The interior is a gigantic Renaissance hall, 20m (66ft) wide, with a barrel vaulted ceiling; at the time of its construction only St Peter's in Rome was larger.

The nearby fountain, the **Richard Strauss-Brunnen**, with its sculpture group from the opera *Salome*, commemorates Munich's best-known musician, the composer of world-famous operas, lieder and tone poems.

KARLSPLATZ AND ENVIRONS

Karlstor, a city gate dating from the 14th century, links Neuhauser Strasse to the busy Karlsplatz, which is popularly known as Stachus after an innkeeper named Eustachius Föderl. Stachus conceals a veritable city of underground shops, which extends from the exit of the U- and S-Bahn station.

Walk north to Lenbachplatz and you'll find the city's loveliest fountain, the late-19th-century **Wittelsbacher Brunnen**, which was built in neo-baroque style by Adolf von Hildebrand. Pacellistrasse, to the east of Lenbachplatz, takes you past the baroque facade of the **Dreifaltigkeitskirche** (Trinity Church). In 1704 a young girl, Anna Maria Lindmayr, dreamt that Munich would be invaded and destroyed unless a new church were constructed. Sure enough, the next year, during the War of the Spanish Succession, Austrian soldiers arrived. Although work on the Dreifaltigkeitskirche did not begin until 1711, the town was saved from destruction.

THE RESIDENZ AND SURROUNDINGS

Max-Joseph-Platz is named after the king whose statue sits in the centre: the fourth Max-Joseph of the Wittelsbach dynasty and the first, thanks to Napoleon, to be king. The statue was put alongside the greatest monument of Max-Joseph's family, the Wittelsbach **Residenz** ❿. In 1385 the citizenry revolted, driving the dukes to construct safer lodgings than the Alter Hof. More than five centuries later, in 1918, another group of rebellious citizens pounded on the Residenz doors during the revolution that resulted in the short-lived Bavarian Socialist Republic. The Wittelsbachs had to move out once again, this time for good.

The Residenz, now a museum, shows just how wealthy the Bavarian principality grew to be. Successive members of the Wittelsbach dynasty expanded the original stronghold to create a complex of palaces around seven courtyards. The Königsbau or King's Tract, bordering the square on the north side, was only built in 1826–35, on the instructions of Ludwig I to house his apartments. Ludwig's architect, Leo von Klenze, adapted the designs of Karl von Fischer to create a heavily rusticated facade with 21 bays in the style of the Florentine Palazzo Pitti.

Before entering the museum through the large central doors, note three other buildings on the square. Opposite stands the neoclassical former **Hauptpostamt**, or Main Post Office, also designed by Klenze. Rebuilt in 1963, the

The elegant Wittelsbacher Brunnen

Nationaltheater, Munich's opera house, closes off the east side of the square. It is a copy of the original building of 1818, a Greek-temple design by Karl von Fischer (first rebuilt by Leo von Klenze after a fire in 1825). Sandwiched between the Residenz and the opera house is the **Residenztheater**, which was built in 1948–51 by Karl Hocheder in place of the Cuvilliés-Theater (see page 46).

Max-Joseph-Platz also marks the beginning of **Maximilianstrasse**, Munich's most elegant avenue, which stretches away towards the River Isar and the brooding presence beyond of the Maximilianeum (see page 63).

RESIDENZMUSEUM AND TREASURY

The **Residenzmuseum** ⓫ (daily Apr–mid-Oct 9am–6pm, mid-Oct–end Mar 10am–5pm, www.residenz-muenchen.de, combination ticket for Residenzmuseum, Schatzkammer and

RESIDENZMUSEUM AND TREASURY

Cuvilliés-Theater available) can be visited independently or as part of a guided tour. There's a huge amount to see in the 112 rooms, halls and galleries, in addition to the 10 rooms of the Schatzkammer (Treasure Chamber). Here are the highlights:

Ahnengalerie (Gallery of the Ancestors). Acquaint yourself with a mere 121 of the Wittelsbachs, starting with Duke Theodor, who lived around AD700.

Antiquarium. Designed by Friedrich Sustris for Duke Albrecht V in 1558, this is the largest and most beautiful Renaissance hall north of the Alps. The room takes its name from the 16th-century busts of ancient Greek and Roman leaders on display.

Porcelain collections. This prodigious array of French, English and German porcelain includes Meissen, from near Dresden, as well as local pieces produced in Nymphenburg. Japanese and Chinese porcelain and superb lacquer work form part of a separate exhibit.

Reiche Zimmer. Together these State Rooms provide the most outstanding example of rococo décor in Germany. Cuvilliés designed them in 1729, and his jewel among jewels was the Grüne Galerie (Green Gallery). The Spiegelkabinett (Cabinet of Mirrors), Miniaturenkabinett and Chinesisches Kabinett are equally fascinating.

Hofkapelle and Reiche Kapelle. Of these intimate chapels, the first was originally set aside for common courtiers, while the second was for the exclusive use of the Wittelsbachs.

Grottenhof. Designed by Sustris in 1581, this is perhaps the most elegant courtyard in the Residenz, distinguished by the graceful arcade along the eastern side and by Hubert Gerhard's fine bronze Perseus fountain set in the middle. The Grottenwand, or Grotto Wall (with a fountain in an alcove), gives the courtyard its name. A statue of Mercury is flanked by Nubian slaves, fish-tailed satyrs, nymphs and parrots, and the ensemble is encrusted with thousands of mussel, scallop and winkle shells.

Schatzkammer (Treasury). A separate exhibition (separate charge) displays dynasty's spectacular collection of jewellery, gold, silver, crystal and enamelware, amassed over the course of 1,000 years. One of the earliest of the Wittelsbach heirlooms is a communion goblet dating from about 890, known as the Arnulfziborium (Arnolph's Ciborium).

THE COURTYARDS AND CUVILLIÉS-THEATER

Apart from the Grottenhof, all the courtyards of the Residenz can be visited free of charge by entering the complex via the older **Maximilian Residenz**, whose early 17th-century facade runs along Residenzstrasse. The most attractive courtyard is the **Brunnenhof**, or Fountain Court, to the right of the entrance, which was built in the shape of a long, stretched octagon in 1620. The Wittelsbach fountain at its centre features Duke Otto von Wittelsbach with four mermen symbolising Bavaria's most important rivers at his feet.

The Cuvilliés-Theater

From the Brunnenhof you can enter the enchanting **Cuvilliés-Theater** ⓘ (separate admission). This rococo gem was originally located where the present Residenztheater stands and found its present location after World War II, when the Brunnenhof layout was reconstructed. Its architect, François de Cuvilliés the Elder, was a dwarf from the Spanish Netherlands, and the theatre is tiny, seating just 450 people. But its sense of festive intimacy turns every performance into a cosy gala. The four-tiered auditorium basks in gilded décor with hosts of Greek nymphs, gods and goddesses, and, with marvellous incongruity, an American Indian girl with her bow and arrows. The acoustics are warm and golden – perfectly suited to the works by Mozart that have been performed here for the past 200 years.

> **Rescue project**
>
> The Cuvilliés-Theater owes its survival to planning and foresight. In 1943, its stucco ornamentation and sculptures were dismantled. Some 30,000 pieces were carried away and stored in the vaults of various castles around Munich. Only six weeks later the theatre was gutted by fire bombs. However, 15 years elapsed before all the pieces were brought out of hiding and reassembled.

ODEONSPLATZ

Residenzstrasse leads out into **Odeonsplatz**, which forms a link between the inner city and Maxvorstadt and the university to the north. If you're coming from Marienplatz, you can also stroll along **Theatinerstrasse**, which is pleasantly pedestrianised and has a number of cafés with outdoor tables. Also look out for the entrance to the **Fünf Höfe** (Mon–Fri 10am–7pm, Sat 10am–6pm; www.fuenfhoefe.de), a high-class shopping arcade with some top names in designer fashion.

Odeonsplatz is dominated on its western flank by the twin towers and dome of the **Theatinerkirche** ⓭ (www.theatiner

kirche.de). This splendid Italian baroque church was built in 1663–8 by two Italian architects, Agostino Barelli and Enrico Zuccalli. The facade was completed later by Cuvilliés. Perhaps because the church was built to celebrate the birth of a baby boy to Princess Henriette Adelaide, a feeling of jubilation animates its rich decoration – with sprigs of ornamental vines, acanthus leaves and rosettes in the most spirited Italian baroque style, and wonderful grey-and-white stucco embellishments in the cupola. Notice, as well, the triumphant pulpit, the high altar and, to the left, the Cajetan altar. This last was dedicated to St Cajetan, founder of the Theatine Order.

Just across the street, facing Odeonsplatz, is the **Feldherrnhalle** (Hall of the Generals), a 19th-century monument to a number of Bavarian military leaders, including the Belgian-born Count Johann Tilly (a hero in the Thirty Years' War) and Prince Karl-Philipp von Wrede, who achieved victory over the French in 1814. Less gloriously, it was the rendezvous for Nazi storm troops in Hitler's unsuccessful putsch of 1923, and was subsequently a focus for marches commemorating the event. Reinforcing the Italian atmosphere of the area, though with less of a light touch, the building is modelled after the Loggia dei Lanzi in Florence.

Looking along Viscardigasse towards the Residenz

At the east side of the square an archway leads through to the Italian Renaissance-style **Hofgarten** (Court Garden), restored and replanted with the chestnut trees, flower beds and fountains specified in the original 17th-century plan. In the centre stands a 12-sided temple dedicated to Diana, topped by a bronze statue of Bavaria. The arcades that line the garden house art galleries and cafés are decorated with frescoes of historic scenes featuring the Wittelsbachs.

LUDWIGSTRASSE

Odeonsplatz leads into **Ludwigstrasse**, which stretches north towards Schwabing (see page 58). This grand avenue of neo-classical buildings, leading into what at the time was nothing but open countryside, was the crown prince, later king Ludwig I's, most eccentric project. He commissioned the buildings as far as Theresienstrasse to the prolific Leo von Klenze; beyond that Friedrich von Gärtner took over with his designs for the Bavarian State Library and the University. An equestrian statue of Ludwig I stands at the beginning of his street, outside Klenze's noble **Leuchtenberg Palais**.

THE MUSEUM QUARTER

KÖNIGSPLATZ

To the northwest of the inner city, beyond the Alter Botanischer Garten, **Königsplatz** ⓮ represents a convergence of the noblest and basest aspirations arising from the past several hundred years of Munich's history. When Ludwig I was still crown prince, he visualised the square as a second Acropolis, a vast open space surrounded by Classical temples. There was no particular reason for the choice of this site (no junction of

The Glyptothek on Königsplatz

roads, for example). Ludwig simply overrode the customary demands of urban planning, and soon had men working on widening the stately Brienner Strasse, the street that took the royal family from the Residenz to Nymphenburg Palace.

With Leo von Klenze working as his architect, Ludwig transformed the square into a grass-covered, tree-lined haven of tranquillity. A hundred years later, Hitler cut down the trees and paved over the grass for the troops and armoured cars of his military parades. (The pompous Nazi Ehrentempel, or Temple of Honour, which stood at the eastern end of the square, was deliberately blown up by the Allied military engineers in 1945.) Today, at last, Königsplatz has returned to its original serenity, and the pastoral greenery is back.

The U-Bahn station brings you out beside the **Propyläen** (Propylaeum), modelled after the entranceway to the Acropolis in Athens. Unlike the original, this splendid monument to

KÖNIGSPLATZ

Ludwig's sublime imperviousness to functional considerations does not lead anywhere, for it closes off Königsplatz rather than providing access to the square. Despite the Doric columns, it's not even authentically Greek, since the central gateway is flanked by two Egyptian-style pylons. The friezes that decorate them show the Wittelsbachs' special attachment to all things Greek: representations of the Greek war of liberation from the Turks, and of the Greek people paying homage to Ludwig's son Otto when he was made their king in 1832.

Situated on the south side of Königsplatz is the **Staatliche Antikensammlungen** (Classical Art Collections; www.antike-am-koenigsplatz.mwn.de, Tue–Sun 10am–5pm; charge), a building

⊙ LEO VON KLENZE

In the early 19th century Munich was transformed from a simple residence city to a truly international centre of art and culture. This is largely down to the collaboration of two men, King Ludwig I, avid art collector and fan of antiquity, and Leo von Klenze, his star architect. Klenze, who was also a noted painter and writer, created a glittering array of neoclassical buildings that cities even twice the size of Munich would have been proud to possess. His projects included the Glyptothek (1815), the rebuild of the Nationaltheater (1823), the Alte Pinakothek (1826), the Königsbau of the Residenz (1826) and the Hauptpostamt (1834). Klenze, along with Friedrich von Gärtner, the sculptor Ludwig Schwanthaler and the painter Peter Cornelius, also gave shape to the Maxvorstadt between Munich and Schwabing, with the elegant Ludwigstrasse as the main axis. He was also active outside Munich, most notably with his work on the New Hermitage in St Petersburg (1839).

The Aeginates in the Glyptothek

which looks rather clumsy with its Corinthian columns set on an excessively elevated pedestal. The displays include a beautiful series of Greek vases and urns and, above all, the highly prized collection of Etruscan gold and silver formed by James Loeb. This German-American benefactor is known to students and scholars through the famous Loebs Classical Library of Greek and Latin texts.

Just across the square stands the companion building, the **Glyptothek** ⓯ (www.antike-am-koenigsplatz.mwn.de, Tue–Sun 10am–5pm, Thur until 8pm). It was designed in 1815 by von Klenze to display Ludwig I's large collection of Greek and Roman sculpture, and was the first building to be planned for use as a public museum. Some 160 pieces, procured on the orders of the king, found a home in the massive, Ionic-columned edifice. The Glyptothek's greatest treasure is the sculpture from the gables of the Temple of Aphaia, found on the Greek island of Aegina. These well-preserved friezes, the *Aeginates*, have been dated to 505BC (west gable) and 485BC (east gable). On them are warriors with their shields, fighting to defend the island's patron goddess. Look for other works of major importance: the *Apollo of Tenea, a Medusa*, the goddess of peace Irene and the *Barberini Faun* (named after a 17th-century Italian family of classicists).

LENBACHHAUS

Before crossing Königsplatz completely, go back through the Propyläen and cross the road to the **Lenbachhaus** ⑯ on Luisenstrasse. This elegant ochre-coloured villa, built in the 1880s in the style of the Florentine Renaissance, was originally the residence of Franz von Lenbach, a wealthy art collector. Today the villa houses the excellent Städtische Galerie im Lenbachaus (Municipal Art Gallery; Tue 10am–8pm, Wed–Sun 10am–6pm; charge) that was expanded and redesigned in 2013 by British architect, Norman Foster. The gallery provides the best overview of Munich painting from the Gothic period to the present day. The most important and popular collections are those from the 19th and 20th centuries including the largest collection of Wassily Kandinsky paintings in Germany, in addition to canvases by Franz Marc, Gabriele Münter, Alexej von Jawlensky, August Macke and Paul Klee. These artists were the members of Munich's pre-World War I *Blaue Reiter* (Blue Rider) school of painting. The name derives from a blue-and-black horseman drawn by Kandinsky for an almanac in 1912. Horses were also a dominant feature of Franz Marc's work. The Lenbachhaus became a gallery for the *Blaue Reiter* collection in 1929. Alongside these works the collections include works by Picasso, Braque, Dalí, the German Expressionists and a distinguished array of contemporary Americans.

Art underground

When the U-Bahn at Königsplatz was built in the late 1970s, an enormous unused space between ground level and the station platforms was created. In 1994 this was converted for use as an art gallery; run as an annexe to the Municipal Gallery in the Lenbachhaus, the Kunstbau hosts prestigious temporary modern art exhibitions.

THE MUSEUM QUARTER

KUNSTAREAL MÜNCHEN

Leave Königsplatz heading north along Arcisstrasse and cross Gabelsberger Strasse to arrive at the Alte Pinakothek, the first of the major museums that make up what is referred to as the Kunstareal München (Munich Art Area; https://kunstareal.de). Visit on Sundays when most museums charge a symbolic €1 admission.

Alte Pinakothek

Devoted to works from the 14th to the 18th centuries, the **Alte Pinakothek** ⑰ (www.pinakothek.de, Tue 10am–8pm, Wed–Sun 10am–6pm; charge) contains some of the world's finest collections of European paintings. It was commissioned by Ludwig I to house the royal art collections, which had been acquired over the centuries by various dukes, electors and Wittelsbach kings. The acquisitions of Ludwig himself form a significant portion of the museum's holdings.

Ludwig chose Leo von Klenze to provide a design for a monumental museum in the style of an Italian Renaissance palace. Ludwig himself laid the foundation stone on 7 April 1826, Raphael's birthday. Badly damaged in the war, reconstruction in 1958 preserved the spacious layout of galleries and introduced some excellent lighting.

The Alte Pinakothek is renowned for its early Dutch as well as early German Old Masters. The

> **State-of-the-art**
>
> When it was opened in 1836, the Alte Pinakothek was the biggest painting gallery in the world. One of the first purpose-built public galleries, it was organised around the different schools of art, and the hanging scheme remains largely the same today.

latter includes Albrecht Dürer's famous *Self Portrait in a Fur Coat* (1500) heralding the arrival of the humanistic spirit of Italy's Renaissance in the medieval north, and his *Four Apostles*, which seems to reflect the turbulent times when the Reformation swept through Northern Europe. Another outstanding German piece is the Altarpiece of the Church Fathers (Kirchenväteraltar), painted in about 1483 by Michael Pacher. Have a look, too, at Albrecht Altdorfer's *Alexanderschlacht* (1529) which portrays Alexander's victory over Darius of Persia. The thousands of soldiers make this a miniaturist masterpiece.

Albrecht Dürer's 'Self-portrait with a Fur Coat', Alte Pinakothek

The scope and quality of the Flemish collection is unique, including as it does one of the world's finest collections of paintings by Peter Paul Rubens. His works, including the *Great Last Judgement* and the *Rape of the Daughters of Leucippus*, hang on the first floor. The Alte Pinakothek is also richly endowed with works by Italian masters: Giotto, Botticelli, Lippi, Ghirlandaio, Perugino, Raphael, Titian, Tintoretto and Tiepolo are all represented, as is Leonardo da Vinci with a small *Madonna with Child* painted when he was only 21. The Dutch are also here with Rembrandt and Franz Hals, and there is Germany's best collection of Spanish paintings, with El Greco, Velázquez and Murillo all represented.

Neue Pinakothek

Opposite the Alte Pinakothek is the **Neue Pinakothek** [18] (www.pinakothek.de/besuch/neue-pinakothek, Thur–Mon 10am–6pm, Wed 10am–8pm; charge). The 'New Gallery' was also founded by Ludwig I to house his collection of contemporary art; the building was destroyed in World War II, however. This elegant sandstone and granite replacement designed by Alexander von Branca opened in 1981. The gallery today contains outstanding works of European art and sculpture from the late 18th to the beginning of the 20th century, ranging from the German Romanticism of Caspar David Friedrich to the Austrian *Jugendstil* of Gustav Klimt. The wonderful collection of French impressionists includes works by Monet, Manet, Degas, Pissaro and Renoir; Cézanne, Gauguin and van Gogh stand for the pioneers of the modern age.

Pinakothek der Moderne

Opposite the Alte Pinakothek is the **Pinakothek der Moderne** [19] (www.pinakothek.de/besuch/pinakothek-der-moderne, Tue–Sun 10am–6pm, Thur until 8pm). Opened in 2002, this is the largest museum of art and design in Europe, bringing Art, Design, Architecture and Work on Paper under one roof in a cutting edge building designed by Stephan Braunfels.

Art. This world-class collection ranges from the main avant-garde movements of the early 20th century to contemporary art. Prominent among the displays, and including some of the 'degenerate art' so despised by the Nazis, are works by artists of *Die Brücke* and the *Blaue Reiter*, and by Max Beckman, who is represented with the largest European collection of his works. Picasso is also represented, as are the surrealists Max Ernst, René Magritte and Salvador Dalí.

Design. A fascinating insight into various design schools from the pioneers of modernism to the present day, focusing

The Neue Pinakothek

on themes such as motor vehicle design, bentwood furniture and computer culture.

Architecture. Focusing mainly on German architecture, the collection includes architectural drawings dating back to the 16th century, as well as photographs, models and computer animations. Look out for works by Balthasar Neumann, Leo von Klenze, Erich Mendelsohn and Le Corbusier.

Work on Paper. The huge collection of prints and drawings is one of the most important in Germany, containing 400,000 works dating from the 15th century to the present.

Museum Brandhorst

The **Museum Brandhorst** [20] (www.museum-brandhorst.de; Tue–Sun 10am–6pm, Thur until 8pm; charge) lends a spectacular new dimension to the Kunstareal, containing stunning contemporary pieces by artists like Cy Twombly, Andy Warhol,

Picasso at the Pinakothek der Moderne

Damian Hirst and Sigmar Polke. The building itself, designed by Sauerbruch Hutton of Berlin, reflects the exquisite art inside, the facade a composition of 36,000 vertical ceramic rods in 23 different colours, with deep tones at the bottom and light pastel shades at the top.

NS-Dokumentationszentrum

The austere edifice of the **NS-Dokumentationszentrum** ㉑ (The Munich Documentation Centre for the History of National Socialism) contains exhibitions commemorating the atrocities of the Nazi apparatus and its consequences up to contemporary times (www.museum-brandhorst.de, Tue-Wed, Fri-Sun 10am–6pm, Thu 10am–8pm; charge). The museum was created in 2015 in the very same place of the former NSDAP headquarters.

SCHWABING

Ludwigstrasse stretches precisely 1km from Odeonsplatz in the south to **Siegestor** (Victory Gate) at its northern end. This triumphal arch was designed for Ludwig I as a monument to the Bavarian army.

Just south of the Siegestor is the **University** and the little square Geschwister-Scholl-Platz, which was named in memory of the brother and sister who were killed with a guillotine by the Nazis for leading an underground resistance movement of students against Hitler's regime. Across the street is **St Ludwig's** (www.st-ludwig-muenchen.de), a neo-romanesque church noted for the gigantic fresco of the *Last Judgement* in the choir, by Peter Cornelius (1836). It is the world's second-largest fresco – measuring 18m (60ft) by 11m (37ft) – after Michelangelo's in the Sistine Chapel in Rome.

LEOPOLDSTRASSE

Siegestor marks the southern boundary of Munich's once bohemian district of Schwabing. Its main shopping street and promenade, **Leopoldstrasse**, has been commercialised by ice-cream parlours, fast-food outlets and bars, but the more idyllic,

⊙ SCHWABING'S HEYDAY

During Schwabing's heyday at the turn of the 20th century, artists and writers flocked to this bohemian area of Munich. Thomas Mann lived here, as did Frank Wedekind and Bertolt Brecht, Wassily Kandinsky and Paul Klee, as well as Franz Marc, Rainer Maria Rilke and symbolist poet Stefan George.

A countess-turned-Bohemian, Franziska zu Reventlow, chronicled the area's free love, free art and freedom for all in her novels. Schwabing was also home to the biting satirical weekly *Simplicissimus* and to the art magazine *Jugend*, which gave its name to *Jugendstil*, the German version of Art Nouveau.

In 1919, the 'Coffeehouse Anarchists', dramatist Ernst Toller and poet Erich Mühsam, took power after the assassination of the prime minister, Kurt Eisner. For all of six days – until the communists pushed the poets out – Schwabing ruled Bavaria, proclaiming the republic a 'meadow full of flowers'.

older part of Schwabing can be discovered easily in the side roads that lead off to the English Garden – Werneckstrasse, for example, or Nikolaiplatz. Ainmillerstrasse, on the west side of Leopoldstrasse, was home to a number of turn-of-the-century painters and writers. Both Ainmillerstrasse and Hohenzollernstrasse (Schwabing's foremost shopping street with its boutiques and arcades) have some magnificent *Jugendstil* facades.

ENGLISCHER GARTEN

From Schwabing, head east to the lovely **Englischer Garten** ㉒. Opened in 1793, the park was the brainchild of an American-born adventurer who had sided with the British in the American Revolution. Better known to the Bavarians as Count Rumford, Benjamin Thompson drew his inspiration from the English landscape gardeners Capability Brown and William Chambers.

⊙ DEGENERATE ART

Hitler's speech inaugurating the Haus der Deutschen Kunst in 1937 attacked the 'obscenities' of avant-garde art and forbade any painter to use colours that the 'normal' eye could not perceive in nature. Two exhibitions were held to distinguish so-called great German art from that designated 'degenerate art'.

The trouble was that the 'degenerate' show was far more popular, and attracted 2 million visitors, five times as many as the other exhibition. Afterwards, many of these paintings, including works by Kandinsky, Mondrian, Kokoschka, and Chagall, were hidden away or sold abroad for valuable foreign currency. Today, some of these works are on display again in the Pinakothek der Moderne.

In fact, the **Chinesischer Turm** (Chinese Tower), a decorative pagoda that functions as a bandstand in the popular beer garden, owes a great deal to Chambers' Cantonese Pagoda in London's Kew Gardens. The natural landscaping is still a joy for visitors, including, famously, the nudists who stretch out along the Eisbach stream in the southern part of the park. The **Monopteros** (love temple) atop a grassy mound south of the Chinese Tower is an attractive focal point from which to admire the city's skyline.

The Monopteros

The gardens stretch almost 5km (3 miles) to the north. Stroll up to the **Kleinhesseloher See**, a boating pond with a café and beer garden on its eastern side; beyond, in the northern part of the park, you can walk beside the River Isar. In the southwest corner is the pretty **Japanese Tea House**, donated by Japan to commemorate the 1972 Olympic Games. Just beyond the Tea House, at Prinzregentenstrasse 1, is the **Haus der Kunst** (House of Art; www.hausderkunst.de, Mon–Sun 10am–8pm, Thur until 10pm; charge), a venue for temporary exhibitions and theatre. Originally called the Haus der Deutschen Kunst, this is another building from the Nazi era. Built as a temple to Hitler's personal vision of a truly German art, the monotonous construction was soon nicknamed the 'Palazzo Kitschi' by Munich wits.

PRINZREGENTENSTRASSE

Further out along Prinzregentenstrasse is the **Bayerisches Nationalmuseum** ❷❸ (www.bayerisches-nationalmuseum.de, Tue–Sun 10am–5pm, Thur to 8pm; charge). Built in 1900, the exterior mirrors the artistic evolution of the periods exhibited inside – a Romanesque east wing, a later Renaissance western facade, a baroque tower and, finally, a rococo west wing. The collection spans German cultural history from the Middle Ages to the 19th century, emphasising both religious and secular arts and craftsmanship. One of the highlights is a collection of wooden sculptures by the Late Gothic master Tilman Riemenschneider.

Now walk across Prinzregentenbrücke, crossing the river to the **Friedensengel** (Angel of Peace), high on her pillar. Begun in 1896, the monument celebrates the 25 years of peace that followed the German defeat of the French in 1871. Portraits of the architects of that peace – Bismarck, Kaisers Wilhelm I and II, and the generals Moltke and von der Tann – decorate the monument. The mosaics of *Peace*, *War*, *Victory* and the *Blessings of Culture* indicate the rather ambiguous nature of the celebration.

There's nothing ambiguous, however, about the **Villa Stuck**, at Prinzregentenstrasse 60, which was built in 1898 for the last in Munich's line of painter-princes, Franz von Stuck. He amassed a fortune rivalling that of Franz von Lenbach by combining the new artistic trends of *Jugendstil* symbolism with the prevailing salon taste. His opulent villa is the perfect setting for the **Jugendstil Museum** (www.villastuck.de, Tue–Sun 11am–6pm; charge) which is housed here. All the interior decoration and furniture date from the turn of the 20th century and the house is often used as a venue for temporary exhibitions.

ALONG THE ISAR

South of the Friedensengel, the banks of the River Isar make for a pleasant stroll. Paths wind their way through parkland and along boardwalks just above the river. Above the Maximiliansbrücke looms the imposing neo-Romanesque facade of the **Maximilianeum**. Completed in 1874, the building was first the home of the Maximilianeum Foundation for Gifted Bavarian Students before becoming seat of the Bavarian Parliament in 1949. At the other side of the bridge, elegant **Maximilianstrasse** leads towards the city centre. The street is named after its creator, Maximilian II (1848–64), who had it lined with buildings designed in a unique Gothic-Renaissance style known as the 'Maximilian style'. Notable structures include the **Völkerkundemuseum**

The Maximilianeum

(Ethnology Museum) and the **Upper Bavarian Government** building opposite; closer into town, at the other side of the inner ring road, is the renowned **Hotel Vier Jahreszeiten**; at this point, before Max-Josef-Platz, Maximilianstrasse becomes Munich's most elegant shopping street.

East of the Maximilianeum is the district of **Haidhausen**. At one time this was a poor working-class area, but it now rivals Schwabing as Munich's trendiest quarter, with pleasant streets and plenty of good eateries and nightspots.

DEUTSCHES MUSEUM

Below Gasteig, the path along the Isar passes the **Müller'sches Volksbad,** the oldest public baths in Munich completed in 1901. With its opulent *Jugendstil* décor, it's a fine place for a swim and sauna.

To the south, across the bridge and occupying its own river island, stands the **Deutsches Museum** ㉔ (daily 9am–5pm; www.deutsches-museum.de; charge). With an exhibition area of over 5 hectares (12.5 acres), this is Europe's largest museum of science and technology. It was established by the engineer Oskar von Miller in 1903, and opened on its present, purpose-built site in 1925. From the outset, the intention was to entertain as well as educate, so the museum is not just a series of static displays, but features many interactive models, experimental machines and audio-visual effects.

Gasteig

At the edge of Haidhausen, above the River Isar, is the **Kulturzentrum am Gasteig**. Opened in 1985, this is one of the premier cultural venues in the city. It has a variety of concert halls and theatres, and is home to the acclaimed Munich Philharmonic Orchestra.

Planes at the Deutsches Museum

It would take days if not weeks to see everything in the museum, which is divided into sections for the various classical fields of technology such as mining, road and bridge building, metallurgy and marine navigation, as well as forms of overland transport – from the carriage to the car. Here you can see the world's first automobile – the Benz Welding three-wheeler. Train enthusiasts will love the first German *Lokomobil*, built in 1862 and still operating. British visitors may note with interest that the Germans have on display a replica of *Puffing Billy*, one of the earliest English locomotives, dating from 1813. The Power Machinery section is also very popular, with its collection of impressive engines and turbines. The Marine Navigation department covers everything from the earliest dug-out canoes to developments in modern shipbuilding, the highlight being the 19th-century fishing boat *Maria*, exhibited alongside an Arab *dhow*.

The first floor is dominated by the department of Aeronautics: ordinary balloons, helicopters and jet aeroplanes are exhibited beside celebrities such as Lilienthal's original glider and the legendary Junkers Ju 52, plus an A4 rocket which forms a link with the department of Astronautics. On this floor also, the departments of Physics and Chemistry provide plenty of interactive materials, along with historical artefacts such as the telescope used to discover Neptune. Also worth a look are the Musical Instruments and Automata exhibition and, on the second floor, an exact replica of the prehistoric paintings of the Altamira Cave in Spain.

OUTSIDE THE CITY CENTRE

SCHLOSS NYMPHENBURG

Away from the heat of the Residenz in the city centre, **Schloss Nymphenburg** (daily Apr–mid-Oct 9am–6pm, mid-Oct–Mar 10am–4pm; www.schloss-nymphenburg.de; charge) was the Wittelsbachs' summer refuge. The gleaming palace is set in extensive grounds with fountains, ponds and four garden pavilions. Tram 17 will get you there.

Together with the Theatinerkirche (see page 47), it was built to celebrate the birth of a new son and heir, Maximilian Emanuel, to Princess Henriette Adelaide in 1662. The palace had modest beginnings as a small summer villa, but it grew over the next century as each succeeding ruler added another wing or his own pavilion.

The palace is approached by a long canal with avenues on either bank leading to a semicircle of lawns, the Schlossrondell, which is the site of the building containing the Royal Porcelain Factory (see page 93). In the central edifice of the palace

SCHLOSS NYMPHENBURG

proper are galleries of fine 18th-century stucco work and ceiling frescoes. The majestic two-storey banquet hall, **Steinerner Saal** (Stone Hall), contains some impressive frescoes by Johann Baptist Zimmermann on the theme *Nymphen huldigen der Göttin Flora* (Nymphs Pay Homage to the Goddess Flora).

To the south, the first pavilion is the home of the famous **Schönheitsgalerie** (Gallery of Beautiful Women). Ludwig I commissioned Joseph Stieler to paint these portraits of Munich's most beautiful young women, including Ludwig's mistress, the dancer Lola Montez.

The **Marstallmuseum**, a dazzling collection of state coaches has been installed in the south wing, in what was once the royal stables. Starting from the extravagance of Karl Albrecht's 18th-century coronation coaches, the vehicles went on to

Schloss Nymphenburg

achieve a state of ornamental delirium under Ludwig II. Look for his Nymphenschlitten (Nymph sleigh), designed for escapades in the Alps. On the first floor is the beautiful **Bäuml** collection of Nymphenburg porcelain, covering examples of the entire output from the Nymphenburg factory, from the early days in the 18th century to the 1920s.

Also in the Nymphenburg palace is the extensive **Museum Mensch und Natur** (Man and Nature Museum; Tue–Fri 9am–5pm, Thur until 8pm, Sat–Sun 10am–6pm; www.mmn-muenchen.de; charge), which covers the history of the planet and life on earth. The position of man in the universe and his responsibilities towards the environment are important themes, and numerous ecological topics are explored, such as population growth and hunger.

The gardens were originally laid out in a subdued Italian style for Henriette Adelaide, but later lost some of their formality. Off to the left lies the **Amalienburg**, built in 1734-9 by François de Cuvilliés, with the help of sculptor Joachim Dietrich and stucco artist Johann Baptist Zimmermann. Wander round the rooms where the hunting dogs and rifles were kept, the Pheasant Room next to the blue and white Dutch-tiled kitchen and, above all, enjoy the

Steinerner Saal ceiling

brilliant silver and pastel-yellow rococo **Spiegelsaal** (Hall of Mirrors), originally the pavilion's entrance.

Continue west to find the **Badenburg** (Bath Pavilion), fitted with fine Delft china fixtures. The **Grosser See** is a large pond dotted with islands; overlooking it is a love temple modelled after Rome's Temple of Vesta, goddess of fire. North of the central canal, with its spectacular cascade of water, is another, smaller pond. On the far side of it stands the **Pagodenburg**, an octagonal tea pavilion. The fourth of the park's pavilions is the **Magdalenenklause** (Hermitage), built for Maximilian Emanuel in 1725. Don't be surprised that the building is a crumbling ruin; the cracks and flaking plaster were deliberately incorporated into the mock Romanesque and Gothic structure, and a Moorish minaret was thrown in too.

> **Allianz Arena**
>
> Fröttmaning, in the north of the city, is home of the 66,000-seat Allianz Arena, built for the 2006 World Cup and as the new home ground for the city's two football teams, FC Bayern München and TSV 1860 München. Its futuristic design enables it to change colour according to which team is playing. To get there take the U6 from Marienplatz.

OLYMPIAPARK

In the north of the city, best accessed via the U-Bahn (U3 from Marienplatz), is the sport and recreation area of the **Olympiapark** (Olympic Park; www.olympiapark.de/de), created for the 1972 Olympic Games. The complex is dominated by the 290m (950ft) high **Olympiaturm**, a symbol of the games. The restaurant and observation decks provide spectacular views of the city and surroundings, and on a clear day the Alps can seem almost close enough to touch. The other major feature of the complex is the **Olympiastadion**, with its 78,000 seating capacity and extraordinary tent-roof structure. This used to be the home of Bayern Munich.

Nearby stands the distinctive main headquarters of BMW. The bowl-shaped building in front is the **BMW Museum** (Tue–Sun 10am–6pm; www.bmw-welt.com/de/location/museum/concept.html), which provides a fascinating insight into the history of the Bavarian Motor Works, with exhibits of cars, motorcycles and aircraft engines. The futuristic **BMW Welt** showroom complex is another worthwhile attraction.

INTO BAVARIA

The Bavarian countryside is at its most beautiful to the south of the city. This is where the plane of southern Bavaria slams into the high Alps, a landscape of dramatic peaks, picturesque lakes, onion-domed churches, tradition-hugging villages and Ludwig II's crazy 19th-century castle follies. Another attractive aspect of the region is that it's easily accessible by public transport, with the S-Bahn and regional trains servicing most major attractions.

To the east and northeast of Munich runs the Romantic Road (Romantisches Strasse), a 350km-long tourist route between Würzburg in the north and Füssen in the south, taking in some of Germany's most idyllic medieval walled towns and blockbuster sights along the way. Most points on the route are accessible by public transport from Munich, though you may need a car to visit some of the more obscure locations.

Also to the east (and a stop on the Romantic Road) is Augsburg, a fascinating medieval town that once rivalled Munich in wealth and importance. Further afield, the varied cities of Nuremberg and Regensburg make for intriguing trips into Bavaria's northern and eastern reaches.

An autumnal Königssee, near Berchtesgaden

NEUSCHWANSTEIN

To reach Bavaria's (and arguably Germany's) most famous attraction, Neuschwanstein Castle, first follow the A96 and B12 to **Landsberg am Lech** (with its interesting medieval town centre), and then take the B17, the Deutsche Alpenstrasse (German Alpine Road). Stop off at Steingaden to visit the lovely **St Johann Baptist Church**, which retains much of its 12th-century Romanesque exterior. You'll also enjoy the pleasant walk in the old cloister. From Steingaden, it's worth making a detour just to the east of the B17 to visit the magnificent **Wieskirche** ㉕ (Apr–Oct daily 8am–8pm, Nov–Mar daily 8am–5pm; www.wieskirche.de), a pilgrimage church dating from 1754 and designed by Dominikus Zimmermann. The ceiling is decorated with a sublime fresco by his brother Johann Baptist, which depicts Christ dispensing divine mercy. In its architecture and decoration, the church is a consummate work – perfect to the last rococo detail and well deserving of its Unesco world cultural heritage status.

Return to the main road for the journey to **Neuschwanstein Castle** ❷⓺ (follow the signs to the castle or look for signs to Füssen; Apr–early Oct daily 8am–5pm, early Oct–Mar daily 9am–3pm; www.neuschwanstein.de; charge). A visit in 1867 to the medieval castle of Wartburg in Thuringia first fired Ludwig's imagination with a vision of the Minnesänger, the minstrels of the 12th century, and he decided to build a castle that would recapture the aura of that romantic era. Ludwig replaced a ruined mountain retreat of his father's in the Schwangau with an extraordinary white-turreted castle. Set in the midst of a forest of fir and pine, it overlooks the gorge of Pöllat and Lake Forggen. Tours include the magnificent throne room, and you can try to imagine, as did Ludwig, the minstrel contests of another age in the Sängersaal. Ludwig II was Wagner's biggest patron and fans of the composer's works will recognise the sculptural and painted allusions to *Tannhäuser*, *Die Meistersinger von Nürnberg* and *Tristan und Isolde*.

While Neuschwanstein castle was being built (it was never completed as Ludwig died when it was only half finished), Ludwig kept an eye on its progress from the neighbouring castle of **Hohenschwangau**, just 1km (0.5 miles) away. This neo-Gothic building had been constructed by his father, Maximilian II. In fact, Neuschwanstein and Hohenschwangau collectively are known as 'die Königsschlösser'. Take a look at the music room,

Castle tickets

Tickets for both Neuschwanstein and Hohenschwangau must be purchased at the Ticket-Center in Hohenschwangau, showing the exact admission times. Online tickets are also available (www.hohenschwangau.de).

with its display of Wagner memorabilia (the composer stayed at Hohenschwangau) and Ludwig's bedroom, noted for its star-studded ceiling.

The third attraction here is the new and impressive **Museum of the Bavarian Kings** (daily 9am–5pm; www.hohenschwangau.de) housed in a former hotel on the shores of the scenic Alpsee lake, a short walk from the Neuschwanstein/Hohenschwangau ticket office. The interior, filled with refracted light from the lake, tells the story of the Wittelsbachs' 700-year tenancy of the Bavarian throne, though due to the museum's location the focus is naturally on Maximilian II and his son, Ludwig II.

If you want to reach the castles from Munich by public transport, take an early train from the Hauptbahnhof to Füssen, then change to local bus or taxi for the short ride out of town.

Neuschwanstein Castle

OBERAMMERGAU AND LINDERHOF

To reach the second of Ludwig's dream castles, take the Garmisch-Partenkirchen Autobahn from Munich, turning off west to **Ettal**. This lovely Benedictine monastery is set in a gently curving valley. Stop and admire Johann Jakob Zeiller's 18th-century fresco of the life of St Benedict. Continue from there to **Oberammergau** ㉗, setting for the world-famous 10-yearly Passion Play, inaugurated in the plague year of 1633 and still

Oberammergau

performed by local people. The Passion Play Theatre, where the epic is staged, can be visited on guided tours. In the town are preserved some very attractive 18th-century facades, adorned with paintings by the so-called *Lüftlmaler* (air painter), Franz Zwinck.

A short ride (or pleasant 12km/7.5 mile hike) west of Oberammergau, Ludwig's favourite castle, remote little **Linderhof** (Apr–mid-Oct daily 9am–6pm, mid-Oct–Mar 10am–4pm; www.schlosslinderhof.de; charge), was the embodiment of his baroque fantasies. The palace, inspired by Versailles, is opulent inside and out. Quite apart from the carefully tailored landscape of pond and park, you could be excused for thinking that the whole romantic Alpine backdrop had been created from Ludwig's imagination. Only the Venus Grotto, carved out of the mountainside and forming another Wagnerian motif from *Tannhäuser*, is in fact man-made.

Oberammergau is one hour 50 minutes by train from Munich Hauptbahnhof with a change in Murnau. Regular local buses link Oberammergau with Linderhof and Ettal.

THE LAKES

Ammersee ㉘ (35km/56 miles southwest of Munich on the A96) is a delightful place for long walks along the lake or up into the wooded hills. Make for the Benedictine Abbey of

Andechs (www.andechs.de) that overlooks Ammersee from the east. The 15th-century church was redecorated in the rococo style by Johann Baptist Zimmermann. The monks still brew first-rate beer (Andechser) here and the monastery runs a very popular beer hall and garden.

To reach Ammersee, take the S8 to Herrsching (€7.80). The trip takes 50 minutes.

The **Starnberger See** ㉙, the northern tip of which is just 22km from Munich city centre, is one of the most popular day trips for city dwellers looking to escape the stifling urban heat. The town of **Starnberg** on the northern shore is just a jumping

⊙ THE BAVARIAN ALPS

On a clear day, particularly during *Föhn*, the Alps provide a stunning backdrop to the Bavarian countryside and are a playground for hikers and climbers, skiers, paragliders and even sailors and windsurfers. Though lower than some of the mountains in neighbouring Austria, they are nonetheless impressive, with steep limestone ridges running from west to east. In the west they begin with the lower **Allgäu Alps**, where Neuschwanstein is located, but these soon give way to the highest section, the Wetterstein range, which culminates in Germany's highest mountain, the **Zugspitze**. Its 2,962m/9,718ft summit can be reached by cable car or the Zugspitzbahn railway from **Garmisch**. A break in the mountains is occupied by the picturesque town of **Mittenwald**, above which rise the impressive **Karwendel Mountains** (mostly in Austria). Further to the east, just beyond Chiemsee, the most spectacular scenery of all can be found around **Berchtesgaden** with the east face of the mighty Watzmann (2,713m/ 8,901ft).

off point for the lake measuring 20km (12 miles) from north to south. Relax in the area's quiet, rural scenery and wander along the peaceful rush-fringed shoreline or hike the five kilometres along the lake edge to Schloss Berg on the eastern side, where in 1886 Ludwig II was found drowned with his doctor in just a few feet of water. It remains a mystery how this came to pass; a dramatic cross rises out of the water to mark the spot. Starnberg can be reached on the S6 (€5.60) in 30 minutes.

Chiemsee ㉚ (70km/43 miles southeast of Munich) is the largest lake in Bavaria and the location of Ludwig II's most ambitious castle. **Herrenchiemsee** (Apr–Oct daily 9am–6pm, Nov–Mar daily 9.40am–4.15pm; www.herrenchiemsee.de; charge) is situated on an island, the Herreninsel, at the western end of the lake and reached by ferry. Ludwig started work on it in 1878, but ran out of money and time, in 1886. Nevertheless, he made a valiant attempt at recreating the grandeur of Versailles, and the magnificent **Spiegelsaal** (Hall of Mirrors) can certainly bear comparison with the Galerie des Glaces. The building, few can fail to notice, pays ample homage to the king Ludwig admired most, Louis XIV. On a tiny island nearby is **Frauenchiemsee** where Duke Tassilo III founded a Benedictine convent in 782. As well as the former convent there are some charming little fishing cottages and restaurants.

Using trains from the Hauptbahnhof, head to Prien (one hour) from where ferries to the Herreninsel depart.

BERCHTESGADEN

Once a favourite summer retreat of the Bavarian royal family, the delightful small town of **Berchtesgaden** and its surroundings encapsulate all the attractions of the Bavarian Alps. Painted houses, a small royal palace and wonderful views contribute to the allure of the town, which is also the

Dawn breaks over Chiemsee

home of the **Nationalparkhaus** (www.nationalpark-berchtesgaden.de), the interpretive centre for the national park which protects the area's sublime but vulnerable landscape. The town's ancient prosperity depended on salt, and visitors can enjoy a thrilling trip into the depths of the old salt mines, the **Salzbergwerk** (May–Oct daily 9am–5pm, Nov–Mar daily 11am–3pm, Apr 10am–3pm; www.salzzeitreise.de; charge). Another trip is up the mountain road to the **Kehlsteinhaus**, also known as the 'Eagle's Nest', Hitler's perch atop the 1,834m (6,017ft) Kehlstein, and now a panoramic restaurant (May to October). Near the foot of the mountain is the **Dokumentation Obersalzberg** (Apr–Oct daily 9am–5pm, Nov–Mar Tue–Sun 10am–3pm; www.obersalzberg.de), an information centre documenting the area's Third Reich connections. But the essential excursion in this area is aboard one of the eco-friendly electric boats that cruise the crystal-clear turquoise waters of the **Königssee** ㉛, affording views of Germany's second-highest mountain, the Watzmann (2,713m/8,900ft), and tying up along the much-photographed onion-domed church of **St Bartholomä**. From here mountain trails lead into some dramatic mountainscape; the best walk is a 6km/4 mile easy-going there-back hike to the **Eiskapelle**, a huge ice cavern.

With your own wheels, Berchtesgaden is an easy day trip from Munich along the A8 motorway (and an even easier one from Salzburg just across the border with Austria). By train from Munich's Hauptbahnhof the trip takes between two and a half to three hours with a change in Freilassing.

NORTH OF MUNICH

Dachau (17km/11 miles northwest of Munich) used to be known primarily for the remains of a 16th-century château and its fine 18th-century facades. Then, on 20 March 1933, after Hitler had been in power for a mere 48 days, Dachau was designated as the site of the first Nazi concentration camp. Today, while you can still appreciate the charming town centre, the main dark tourism attraction is the **Dachau Concentration Camp Memorial Site** ㉜ (daily 9am–5pm; www.kz-gedenkstaette-dachau.de) which occupies the former camp. Exhibitions document the camp's sinister history in a moving and often disturbing way (it's not recommended children visit the museum). Dachau was not an extermination camp but served as a detention centre for political prisoners; even so, 31,951 deaths were recorded between 1933 and 1945. You can see the original crematorium and gas chambers (labelled 'Bad' for showers), built but never used, as well as reconstructed prison barracks.

To reach the concentration camp, take the S2 (€5.60) to Dachau then change onto regular city bus 726, alighting at the KZ-Gedenkstätte stop.

Schloss Schleissheim (Apr–Sept Tue–Sun 9am–6pm, Oct–Mar Tue–Sun 10am–4pm; charge; www.schloesser-schleissheim.de) in Munich's northern suburbs is another worthwhile half-day trip from the city centre. The Neues Schloss has a glorious staircase with frescoes by Cosmas Damian Asam. Beautiful stucco work adorns banqueting halls and galleries such as the Barockgalerie, containing a fine collection of 17th-century Dutch and Flemish paintings. The gardens, complete with waterfall and canals, are a triumph of French landscape design. Make a point of visiting the **Schloss Lustheim** hunting lodge at the eastern end. Nearby stands a branch of the Deutsches Museum, the **Flugwerft Schleissheim** (daily 9am–5pm; www.deutsches-museum.de/en/flugwerft/information; charge) housing an impressive collection of flying machines, a must for children and potential pilots.

The castles and the museum are around 15 minutes' walk from Oberschleissheim S-Bahn station on the S1 line.

Freising is the closest town to Munich Airport, and could fill half a day while waiting for a flight (regular buses run to and from the terminals). Once the seat of the local bishop, the main attraction here is the huge hilltop cathedral dedicated to Sts Maria and Korbinian, the interior of which is another masterly baroque collaboration by the Asam brothers. For some less

The baroque facade of Schloss Schleissheim

sober pleasures, head to the **Staatsbrauerei Weihenstephan** (Mon–Thur 8:30am–4pm, Fri until 3pm; www.weihenstephaner. de), said to be the oldest brewery in the world. Tours end with a 'tasting session'.

Freising station (€8.40) is the last stop on a branch of the S1 that peels off from the main line to the airport at Neufarhn.

THE ROMANTIC ROAD

Stretching for 350km from the vineyards of Würzburg to the foothills of the Alps at Füssen, the **Romantic Road** (Romantische Strasse) is Germany's most popular tourist route. You could spend a month exploring this string of perfectly preserved medieval walled towns, hilltop castles, mighty cathedrals and pretty churches, and all but the most remote of the sights are just a short train ride (or two) from Munich Hauptbahnhof. The stopping-off points along the route form some of the most enchanting outings from the Bavarian capital.

Würzburg ㉝ marks the start of the Romantic Road's journey south. This city on the River Main was once the seat of the Prince-Bishops, one of whom, Schönborn, enjoyed a lavish lifestyle in the magnificent, Unesco-listed **Residenz** (Apr–Oct daily 9am–6pm, Nov–Mar 10am–4.30pm; www.residenz-wuerzburg. de; charge) built for him by the famous central European architect, Balthasar Neumann. This is one of the largest and most flamboyant baroque palaces in Germany, boasting a succession of opulent interiors and, crowning the huge staircase, the largest ceiling painting in the world, the work of the Venetian artist Tiepolo. At the centre of the Franconian vineyards, Würzburg has a relaxed atmosphere. There's a winery in the late-medieval hospice known as the Juliusspital, and a tour of the wine-producing villages along the Main is highly recommended, as is a visit to the Prince-Bishops' baroque summer palace at

Veitshöchheim (garden: daily dawn–dusk; palace: Apr–Sep Tue–Sun 9am–6pm, Oct–Mar 10am–4pm; www.schloesser.bayern.de; charge), 7km (4 miles) from Würzburg. This is the country's most famous rococo garden, decorated with more than 200 statues.

Würzburg is 280km from Munich along the A3 and A9 motorways. The train journey takes just two hours.

Rothenburg ob der Tauber in the old town

Rothenburg ob der Tauber ❹ is an essential stop along the way, its quaint name matching the little medieval city's perfect state of preservation. By blanking out the crowds of visitors wandering the streets, relaxing in the main square, or filing along the sentry-walk running the whole length of the 2.5km (1.5 mile) fortifications, it's easy to imagine oneself transported magically back into an idealised Bavaria of the Middle Ages. There's a wonderful overall view from the tall tower of the Renaissance Rathaus over Rothenburg's red-tiled rooftops to the lovely Franconian countryside. A stroll around the streets reveals an almost endless succession of delightful townscapes, none more photographed than the **Plönlein**, a cobbled space of changing levels framed by towers and half-timbered houses.

Rothenburg ob der Tauber is a feasible day trip from Munich by car, but the train journey requires two changes (at Treuchtlingen and Steinach) and takes over three hours.

> **Down in one**
>
> Rothenburg was spared from destruction in the Thirty Years' War when its mayor successfully downed a 3.25 litre (nearly 6 pint) draught of wine in one gulp, a seemingly impossible feat, recreated each year at the Meistertrunk Festival in late May.

Dinkelsbühl ⑤ is another picturesque town, with intact defences, pastel-hued townhouses, a fine parish church and slightly fewer visitors. It also escaped obliteration during the Thirty Years' War when its children appealed en masse to a besieging general. The event is recreated at the annual Kinderzeche festival. A day trip to Dinkelsbühl is only possible if you have your own car.

Nördlingen, is also a well preserved medieval town sporting intact ramparts interspersed with 16 towers and five gateways, but has a slightly more workaday feel and far fewer visitors than Rothenburg. The top sight here is the unique **Rieskrater Museum** (May–Oct Tue–Sun 10am–4.30pm, Nov–Apr Tue–Sun 10am–noon and 1.30pm–4.30pm; www.rieskrater-museum.de) devoted to explaining the story of the 25km (16 mile) diameter crater, formed by a giant meteorite 15 million years ago, at the centre of which the town lies. A treat for steam train buffs is the **Bayerisches Eisenbahnmuseum** (Bavarian Railway Museum; Mar, Apr and Oct Sat noon–4pm, Sun 10am–5pm, May–Sept Tue–Sat noon–4pm, Sun 10am–5pm; www.bayerisches-eisenbahnmuseum.de; charge) displaying various German locos from down the ages. Summer steam specials run north to Dombühl (via Dinkelsbühl) and Gunzenhausen.

Nördlingen can be reached by train in 2.5 hours from Munich's Hauptbahnhof with a change in Donauwörth.

THE ROMANTIC ROAD

Burg Harburg 36 (hourly tours in German Apr–Oct Tue–Sun 10am–5pm; http://burg-harburg.de) is arguably the Romantic Road's most dramatic castle, rising from a wooded hilltop with views of the tranquil countryside for miles around. The 11th-century stronghold was remodelled in the 18th century and the interior holds collections of tapestry, gold and silver.

Harburg is two hours by train from Munich with a change in Donauwörth ten minutes away. A visit is best combined with half a day in Donauwörth.

Donauwörth may not be the most popular stop-off on the Romantic Road, but this attractive town at the confluence of the Danube and Wörnitz river is definitely worth half a day's perusal. The 13th century **Rathaus** (town hall) has a carillon that puts on daily performances at 11am and 4pm. At the other

The dramatic Burg Harburg

end of Reichstrasse, the main thoroughfare, the 15th-century **Liebfraukirche** has an unusual sloping floor and a climbable tower affording views as far as the Alps.

Donauwörth is simple to reach by rail with trains making the journey direct from Munich in 90 minutes.

South of Donauwörth the next stop on the Romantic Road is Augsburg. About 90km/56 miles south of Augsburg is the baroque Wieskirche (see page 71). The Romantic Road comes to a fitting climax at the gates of Neuschwanstein Castle (see page 72).

AUGSBURG

Founded in 15BC and named after Emperor Augustus, **Augsburg**, 50km (31 miles) from Munich, had its heyday in the late Middle Ages, when the Fugger family made it Central Europe's banking centre. Their **Fuggerei** (Apr–Sept daily 8am–8pm, Oct–Mar daily 9am–6pm; www.fugger.de), a gated complex of old people's homes, was the first of its kind in the world, and is still home to deserving pensioners. With streets and squares beautified by Renaissance fountains and lined with fine townhouses, Augsburg is a stately city, its pride and wealth on ostentatious display in the Golden Hall of the **Rathaus** and in the sumptuous furnishings and fittings of the cathedral. Augsburg is 42 minutes by rail from Munich's main station.

REGENSBURG AND AROUND

As one of the country's largest cities to have remained unscathed by war, **Regensburg** ③, 130km (81 miles) north of Munich, has many historical delights. Founded by the Romans to guard their frontier on the Danube, in the Middle Ages it was the biggest city in Bavaria, and has kept a wealth of ancient buildings lining the grid pattern of streets and alleyways established by the Romans. Unique in Germany are the fortified tower houses built by prosperous medieval merchant families to flaunt their wealth and status; some 30 of these extraordinary structures have survived. Another remarkable survivor is the **Steinerne Brücke** (Stone Bridge), a 15-span marvel of medieval engineering thrown across the Danube in the mid-12th century. From the bridge there is a fine prospect of the city still looking much as it must have done in the Middle Ages; beyond the gateway and clock tower guarding the bridge approach rises Regensburg's **Dom** (Cathedral), the finest Gothic structure in Bavaria, begun in the 13th century and completed in the 19th with the addition of delicate openwork spires. Its sculpture of the 'Laughing Angel' is famous, as is its array of stained glass.

The city's most illustrious family was the princely dynasty of Thurn and Taxis, pioneers in the 16th century of a reliable postal service. The opulent lifestyle they enjoyed is on show in the **Schloss Thurn und Taxis** (guided tours only – check website for times; www.thurnundtaxis.de). The tour also takes in lovely medieval cloisters.

High above the Danube a short distance downstream from Regensburg stands the gleaming white neo-Grecian temple of **Walhalla** (daily Apr–Oct 9am–5.45pm, Nov–Mar 10am–11.45am, 1–3.45pm; www.schloesser.bayern.de/deutsch/schloss/objekte/

Regensburg

walhalla.htm), built by King Ludwig I of Bavaria in 1842 to honour Germany's heroes.

Its array of more than 120 busts begins with the 10th century King Henry the Fowler, and it is still being added to; the latest to be honoured is Sophie Scholl, the Munich student executed by the Nazis for her resistance to the regime.

Regensburg is one hour 20 minutes by train from Munich and less than two hours up the A9 and A93 by car.

NUREMBERG

Lovingly rebuilt after wartime devastation, the Altstadt in Nürnberg (Nuremberg) conveys the atmosphere of the archetypal German medieval city, with formidable defensive walls, streets lined with red-roofed old buildings, squares presided over by great Gothic churches and fabulous fountains. Overlooking it all from a rocky summit is an Imperial castle. The unchallenged capital of northern Bavaria, **Nuremberg** ❸ is associated not just with emperors and Wagner's Mastersingers, but also with some of the grimmer aspects of Nazism, in particular the ostentatious pageantry of party rallies and the postwar trials of the Third Reich's leaders.

The Altstadt is divided into roughly equal halves by the River Pegnitz, which is spanned by the picturesque **Heilig-Geist-Spital**, a 15th-century almshouse. To the south, the twin-towered **Lorenzkirche** (Church of St Lawrence) contains masterworks by the great craftsmen the city nurtured at its zenith in the 15th and early 16th centuries, as does the lovely **Frauenkirche** (Church of Our Lady) to the north. The Frauenkirche has a glockenspiel with performing automata, while the marketplace it occupies is the scene of the Christkindlmarkt, Nuremberg's world-famous Christmas market. Here too is the 19m (62ft) Gothic **Schöner Brunnen**, the city's foremost fountain, with an astonishing array of statuary. From here, Burgstrasse leads upwards past the Sebaldskirche and Rathaus to the **Kaiserburg** (Imperial Castle; daily Apr–Sept 9am–6pm, Oct–Mar 10am–4pm; www.kaiserburg-nuernberg.de), a complex structure begun in the 12th century by Emperor Frederick Barbarossa. From the main tower there is a fine panorama over the Altstadt. Below the castle is the **Albrecht Dürer Haus** (Tue–Fri 10am–5pm, Thur 10am–8pm, Sat and Sun 10am–6pm, July–Sept and Dec Mon 10am–5pm; www.museen.nuernberg.de/duererhaus), the residence of Nuremberg's most famous son. Some of the artist's finest work can be seen in the enormous **Germanisches Nationalmuseum** (Tue–Sun 10am–6pm, Wed until 9pm; www.gnm.de; charge, free Wed 6–9pm), whose huge collection of artefacts spans German culture from the earliest time.

Just beyond the city walls, the **DB Museum** (German Railways Museum; Tue–Fri 9am–5pm, Sat–Sun 10am–6pm; www.dbmuseum.de; charge) is the largest of its kind in Germany, with a fine collection of railway artefacts and a huge model railway. Southeast of the centre, some of the monster structures erected for the Nazi Party rallies still stand, notably the incomplete congress centre modelled on Rome's Colosseum.

Trains leave Munich's Hauptbahnhof for Nuremberg regularly (one hour). By car it takes two hours along the A9 motorway.

Half-timbered architecture of the Old Town, Nuremberg

The Philharmonie concert hall at Gasteig

WHAT TO DO

CONCERTS AND OPERA

Munich has no problem in providing entertainment – there's something here to suit every taste. First and foremost, Munich is a city of music, with four major symphony orchestras: the Bavarian State Orchestra, Munich Philharmonic, Bavarian Radio Symphony and Graunke Symphony Orchestra. The main concerts are performed at the **Kulturzentrum am Gasteig**, an enormous complex that incorporates several concert halls under one roof.

In summer there are open-air concerts on Odeonsplatz and Königsplatz, or you can enjoy performances in the palatial setting of Nymphenburg, Blutenburg, or Schleissheim. Music does not stop during the winter, when concerts are performed in the Frauenkirche and many other churches in town.

Opera has long been a Munich attraction. The town vies with Bayreuth for performances of Wagner, and the works of Mozart and Richard Strauss are firm favourites. Though the Italians take second place, Verdi, Rossini and Donizetti are by no means neglected. The Nationaltheater makes every opera evening seem like a gala. The Bavarian State Orchestra plays under the world's greatest conductors, and the summer festival (*Münchner Opernfestspiele*) in July and August attracts the best international singers.

Seasonal venues

A Munich Season (Münchner Saison) from December to February offers the special joy of Mozart operas in the Cuvilliés-Theater. In summer, open-air opera is staged in the pleasant Brunnenhof courtyard of the gigantic Residenz.

Jazz is a favourite in Munich; internationally acclaimed musicians play nightly in many places, most notably at the Unterfahrt im Einstein (www.unterfahrt.de), Einsteinstrasse 42, and at Mister B's (www.misterbs.de), Herzog-Heinrich-Strasse 38, both in Haidhausen. In summer you can also find jazz and dixie musicians playing at the Waldwirtschaft beer garden (www.waldwirtschaft.de).

Munich is a major venue for **rock and pop concerts**, attracting a steady stream of international acts. The biggest bands play in the Olympic Stadium; other venues include the Olympiahalle, the Muffathalle, Schlachthof, Elserhalle and Backstage. The **Tollwood Festival**, Munich's lively outdoor festival of music, theatre and art, held in the southern part of the Olympia Park in June and July, attracts well-known international bands and World Music artists to its concert tent.

To find out what's happening when you're in Munich, get hold of a copy of the monthly programme from the Tourist Office or

NIGHTLIFE

The area around Münchener Freiheit in Schwabing is the best known nightlife district; Feilitzstrasse and Occamstrasse are lined with clubs and pubs. Haidhausen is Munich's other 'in' area. The Glockenbachviertel, located south of Sendlinger Tor, is the focus of the gay scene, and nearby, on the streets radiating from Gärtnerplatz, a large number of hip new bars have opened up. For nightclubs head to behind the Ostbahnhof (Friedenstrasse) where the Kultfabrik (www.werksviertel-mitte.de) houses 29 clubs, bars and eateries and Optimolwerke (www.optimolwerke.de) hosts a further eight nightspots.

In one of the beer tents at the Oktoberfest

visit www.munich-tourist.de; another useful source of information is the monthly English-language magazine, Munich Found (www.munichfound.com).

FESTIVALS

It seems something is always being celebrated in Munich. More than 100 days a year are officially given over to festivals, processions, banquets and street dances commemorating events such as the arrival of the first strong beer of the year (*Starkbierzeit*) or the departure – several centuries ago! – of this plague or that occupying army. In fact, any excuse will do.

Running from January 7, **Fasching** (carnival) is almost as mad in Munich as it is in the Rhineland. Some 2,500 balls are held all over town for policemen and doctors, lawyers and butchers, artists and plumbers. There are masked processions, and market women at the Viktualienmarkt have their special dance at midday on Shrove Tuesday.

The biggest blowout of all is the **Oktoberfest**. This began when the Crown Prince Ludwig (later Ludwig I) celebrated his marriage to Princess Theresa in October 1810 with a horse race, to which everybody turned up. They came again the next year, too, and the year after, and they've been pouring into the city from around the world ever since. Although the horse race has been dropped and the festivities now take place during the warmer second half of September, the blushing bride is not forgotten – the name of the site to the west of the city centre on which the Oktoberfest is held is Theresienwiese (though locals refer to it as the *Wies'n*, which is also a nickname for the festival).

The festival begins with a procession of *Wies'n* brewers and innkeepers with their splendidly decorated beer wagons followed by the one carrying the Festival Queen. For two weeks after the mayor has tapped the first barrel, revellers consume gargantuan quantities of beer, toted around 10 litres at a time by the strong-armed beer maids. This brew washes down huge numbers of barbecued chickens, sausages and spit roasts.

And to work all that off, there's the fun of the fair, with roller coasters, giant Ferris wheel and dodgem cars.

SHOPPING

Munich is an elegant town, the capital of Germany's fashion industry, so there's no lack of chic boutiques, especially on **Theatinerstrasse, Maximilianstrasse,** and on Schwabing's **Leopoldstrasse**. The **Fünf Höfe** (Five Courtyards) shopping precinct between Theatinerstrasse and Kardinal-Faulhaber-Strasse is another ultra-chic address.

Munich is also the place for the world's best selection of

tailored garments (coats, jackets and suits) made in Loden cloth, a Bavarian speciality. This waterproof wool fabric, originally developed for hunters, has kept the people of Munich warm for over a hundred years.

You may even fancy trying on the Bavarian folk costume (*Tracht*). There are smart green-collared grey jackets for men or, for women, brightly coloured *Dirndl* dresses with a full gathered skirt and fitted bodice. *Lederhosen*, those slap-happy traditional shorts for Bavarians, are also widely available.

Nymphenburg porcelain is still turned out in traditional rococo designs. You can view pieces (and make a purchase) at the factory at Schloss Nymphenburg (www.schloss-nymphenburg.de; see page 66) or in the Fünf Höfe (www.fuenfhoefe.de). Connoisseurs should be on the lookout for old Meissen or modern Rosenthal.

Cutlery, kitchen utensils and electronic gadgets are of a very high standard and superbly designed. You might also like to consider linens, in modern or traditional designs, which are renowned for their good old-fashioned quality. A great way to save on winter heating bills is to invest in a sumptuous duck or goose down *Federbett* or eiderdown, another good buy.

Germany remains at the forefront of quality optical equipment manufacture,

Fashion born in Munich: the Escada shop on Theatinerstrasse

> **Auer Dult**
>
> The 'Auer Dult' is a seasonal fleamarket dating back to the 14th century. It takes place over nine days, three times a year (May, July and October) in the Au district (around Mariahilfplatz, south of the Deutsches Museum). There are invariably some interesting bargains to be had.

and its famous-name brands are still very visible in binoculars, cameras and camcorders.

The country has always produced excellent children's toys; its industrial prowess is reflected in the intricate building sets and model trains.

The presence of so many great orchestras and musicians in Germany means that the selection of recorded music here is probably second only to the United States. The production of musical instruments, such as the finest grand pianos, violins, and even harmonicas, also enjoys a venerable reputation.

SPORTS

The city's great boon to sports lovers was the construction of the Olympic facilities in 1972. All year round, ice-skating fans congregate at the Olympic ice rink. The swimming pool at the Olympia Schwimmhalle can be used by anyone, as can about a dozen other indoor as well as open-air pools *(Freibäder)* dotted around the city. The outdoor pools, which open in May, are a summertime institution in Munich; they are superbly maintained and all provide lawns for sunbathing. Most of the indoor pools are equipped with saunas and other wellness facilities; the Cosimabad in Bogenhausen has a wave pool and the award-winning Westbad has a 60m slide. The Dante-Winter-Warmfreibad has a heated outdoor pool, which attracts many people even in snowy winters.

Munich has its share of tennis courts, too: the best are at Olympiapark and in the Englischer Garten.

While serious runners might want to hit the track in the Olympic Stadium, jogging and running in the Englischer Garten is more fun, especially the stretch along the River Isar. Running in the city is also pleasant, as long as you get out early enough (before 7am) to avoid the traffic. For some good exercise and lovely scenery, try cycling the 14km (9 miles) along the river path to Ismaning, or any of the bike routes throughout Munich. For people who don't want to exert themselves, delightful raft trips (Flossfahrten) are organised at weekends. You can drift slowly down the Isar from Wolfratshausen to Munich, while the beer flows and brass bands play. It is recommended to book as early as possible (www.schrall.com).

There are 15 golf courses located within a radius of 20km (12 miles) around the city. Courses in the Munich area include Eichenried, Feldafing, Olching, Wörthsee and Margarethenhof am Tegernsee.

Farther out of Munich you can do some serious sailing or windsurfing on Ammersee, Starnberger See, Tegernsee and Chiemsee. The local lakes and rivers also offer good fishing.

Hiking is a major pastime, especially as you approach the Bavarian

The Müller'sches Volksbad, a wonderful 'Jugendstil' experience

Soaking up the sun at the zoo

Alps. Just 97km (61 miles) from Munich, Garmisch-Partenkirchen provides guides for mountain climbing. There are plenty of peaks to tackle, including the 2,962-m (9,717-ft) high Zugspitze. Once you are in the Alps, the whole range of winter sports is at your disposal. Garmisch has, in addition to skiing (and a very professional ski school), its own Olympic rink for skating and ice hockey. The more sedate can try curling, and for the more adventurous there is a bobsled run.

CHILDREN'S MUNICH

Munich is a wonderful city for children, at any time of year and in any weather. Many of the museums are suitable for children, but the **Deutsches Museum** (www.deutsches-museum.de; see page 64) is the biggest hit by far, with plenty of fascinating machines and models to play with, and hands-on exhibits for children to operate for themselves. Adults can accompany children aged 10 or under to the **Kinderreich** ('Kids' Kingdom') section, where they can explore a variety of scientific phenomena such as light, sound and energy, with many fun activities. Children can build a house with giant building blocks and play water games in WaterWorld.

CHILDREN'S MUNICH

The **Museum Mensch und Natur** (www.mmn-muenchen.de; see page 68) is an excellent museum that explores a variety of issues on the subject of man, nature and ecology, and is full of weird and wonderful exhibits sure to keep youngsters of all ages entertained.

You could also try the **Marionette Collection** in the Stadtmuseum (www.muenchner-stadtmuseum.de; see page 39); the **Deutsches Jagd- und Fischereimuseum** (www.jagd-fischerei-museum.de/start; see page 41), with exhibits on game, hunting techniques, weapons and trophies, and the story of fishing equipment through the ages; and the **Spielzeugmuseum** (see page 32) showing examples from 200 years of toys. **Sea Life** (www.visitsealife.com/de/de/muenchen) in the Olympiapark introduces children to the underwater environment of rivers and seas, while the **BMW Museum** (www.bmw-welt.com/de/location/museum/concept.html) has displays of cars and motorbikes (see page 70).

Last but by no means least, south of the Zoo, at Geiselgasteig, is the **Bavaria Filmstadt** (www.filmstadt.de), which appeals to children and adults alike. Tours daily 10am–5pm.

A DAY AT THE ZOO

For a change from cultural activity, try the delightful **Hellabrunn Zoo** (U3 U-Bahn or bus No 52 to Thalkirchen from Marienplatz; www.hellabrunn.de). Here, animals are grouped according to their continent of origin, and you'll see zoological curiosities such as the tarpan and the white-tailed gnu. The chimps 'working out' in their own gym attract audiences. It's possible to spend hours in the kids' area alone, with pony rides and goat pens, plus a superb adventure playground and suspension bridge.

CALENDAR OF EVENTS

For the most up-to-date information on the city's festivals and arts calendar, including a current list of times and dates, ask the tourist information office for their monthly programme of events, or consult the local press.

7 January to Ash Wednesday Fasching: costumed balls and processions.

Mid-March Starkbierzeit: making and sampling of special strong beers during the week including 19 March (St Joseph's Day), always ending in '-ator' like Salvator.

End of April Frühlingsfest (Spring Fair): funfair, concerts. Auer Dult: fleamarket, over nine days from the last Saturday in April (also in July and Oct).

Mid-June Stadtgründungsfest (Foundation of the City): weekend around the 14th of June.

June Corpus Christi: colourful street procession from the Frauenkirche to Maxvorstadt; people and horses wear traditional costumes.

End of June Filmfest München (Munich Film Festival, last week of June): at selected cinemas and Gasteig Culture Centre.

June/July Tollwood Sommerfestival: a three-week open-air extravaganza of music, art and theatre from around the world, held in the southern part of the Olympiapark. Nymphenburger Schlosskonzerte: concerts in the palace and grounds of Schloss Nymphenburg.

3 weeks in July Opernfestspiele: a variety of opera performances that take place at the Nationaltheater and Cuvilliés-Theater.

September/October Oktoberfest: 16 days up to the first Sunday in October. Commemorates the marriage of Ludwig I to Princess Theresa in 1810. Beer drinking, hog roasts, funfair and processions.

October Munich Marathon: 26.2-mile and 13.1-mile runs through the city with a grandstand finish on the track of the Olympic Stadium.

December Christkindlmarkt (Christmas market): market offering crafts and gifts for the season on and around Marienplatz. Further markets at Münchner Freiheit, Weissenburger Platz and Rotkreuzplatz, and at the Chinese Tower in the English Garden. Tollwood Winterfestival at Theresienwiese.

EATING OUT

Eating and drinking are favourite pastimes in Munich. Conviviality reigns supreme, both in the temples of gastronomy and at the long, communal tables of the *Bräuhaus*, *Gaststätte*, *Gasthaus*, *Wirtschaft* and *Biergarten*.

WHERE TO EAT

With its great prosperity and tradition of good living, Munich has a great deal to offer gastronomically – indeed some of its sophisticated eateries, manned by award-winning chefs, are among the finest anywhere. In addition, the city remains a bastion of traditional Bavarian fare; you can tuck into roast duck, chicken or pork with dumplings at the city's beer gardens, and there are still some very good Bavarian restaurants as well. Time was when international cuisine in Munich was almost exclusively Italian, Greek, Turkish and Balkan, but now you can get just about anything, a recent development being the surge in Asian fare, with some really excellent restaurants.

Munich's growing sophistication is such nowadays that elegance, however casual, is considered to be

A famous Bavarian Bräuhaus

more important than the traditional formality of ties for men or skirts for women. It's a good idea to reserve a table at the smarter places. A service charge of 15 percent is included in the bill, but waiters are given a little extra.

Beer halls and beer gardens

The niceties of dress and advance reservations are not a problem at the more popular *Gaststätte* or *Bräuhaus* – literally meaning 'brewery', but in actual fact a beer hall. These establishments usually serve full meals in addition to beer. All the great breweries have their own beer halls in Munich, and beer gardens, too. Some of the most popular beer gardens are in the Englischer Garten, at the Chinese Tower, at the Hirschau, and beside the Kleinhesseloher See. Flaucher, located on the River Isar to the south of the city centre, is also well worth visiting, as are Taxisgarten and Hirschgarten in the west of the city. You can either bring your own picnic along to the beer garden or choose from an array of traditional specialities served up at the various stands.

Weinstuben (taverns), less numerous in the beer country of Bavaria than in other regions of Germany, serve meals and wine by the glass rather than by the bottle.

In a separate category is the *Konditorei* (a

The beer garden at the Chinese Tower in the English Garden

WHAT TO EAT

café-cum-pastry shop), the bourgeois fairyland where you can spend a whole afternoon reading the newspapers provided. This is the perfect place for a feast of pastry, ice cream, coffee, tea and fruit juices, with a good choice of wines. Most provide a limited selection of light snacks and salads.

> **Main meal**
>
> Many Germans like to eat their main meal in the middle of the day, and generally prefer a lighter supper (*Abendbrot*, or 'evening bread') of cold meats and cheeses, possibly eaten with a salad, in the evening.

WHAT TO EAT

Breakfast
Germans start the day with a meal that is a bit more substantial than the typical 'Continental' breakfast. The distinctive touch is the selection of cold meats – including ham, salami and liver sausage (*Leberwurst*) – and cheese served with the bread. You will find many kinds of bread – brown (rye with caraway seeds), as well as rich black (*Pumpernickel*) and white. If you like boiled eggs, try *Eier im Glas* – two four-minute eggs served whole, already shelled, in a glass dish. And with it all comes tea, hot chocolate or coffee – stronger than the Anglo-American variety, but weaker than French or Italian espresso.

Soups and starters
Bavarians specialise in excellent *Leberknödlsuppe*, a soup made with spicy dumplings of flour, breadcrumbs, beef liver, onions, marjoram and garlic. *Kartoffelsuppe* contains potatoes, celery, leek and parsnip. Other popular soups are made with beans (*Bohnensuppe*) or lentils (*Linsensuppe*), and chunks of sausage.

Radishes and carrots at the Viktualienmarkt

For hors d'oeuvres, try smoked calf's tongue served with horseradish sauce (*Kalbszüngerl mit Meerrettich*) or pork tongue boiled with juniper berries, bay leaves and peppercorns, accompanied by sauerkraut (*Schweinszüngerl im Kraut*).

Bavarian specialities

The pig and the calf dominate Bavarian main dishes, often in combination. Pork or veal can be either pot-roasted (*Kalbs-* or *Schweinebraten*) or grilled on a spit (*am Spiess*) to obtain a marvellous crackling skin. The Munich speciality is spit-roast *Schweinshaxn*, hock of pork, sold in halves or whole. Be careful when ordering – a half is a meal in itself. The ultimate delicious roast is *Spanferkel*, or suckling pig. For a change, sample the excellent game when in season – venison, hare, partridge and pheasant. Venison is often marinated until tender and served with a sauce of sweet raisins or redcurrants, or a purée of chestnuts. Try trout (*Forelle*)–this local freshwater fish is unbeatable if boiled absolutely fresh (*blau*) – or some whitefish (*Renke*), usually fried. Bavarians also like their offal, one popular dish being *Saure Lüngerl* (chopped lung in vinegar sauce), which is best accompanied by a good glass of dry white wine.

Whether you've ordered *Saure Lüngerl* or *Schweinebraten*, your meal will often be accompanied by a large dumpling (*knödel*) or two, either of made of bread (*Semmelknödel*) or potato *(Kartoffelknödel)*; sautéed potatoes *(Bratkartoffeln)* may also be on the menu. Also available is the sweet-and-sour red cabbage, or *Blaukraut*, cooked with apples, raisins, onions, cloves and white vinegar. Plain sauerkraut is often prepared in white wine with juniper berries or caraway seeds. Salads include cucumber salad *(Gurkensalat)*, a good white cabbage salad *(Weisskrautsalat)*, or the excellent potato salad *(Kartoffelsalat)*.

Snacks

Snacks *(Schmankerl)* can be eaten at any time of day. Local people enjoy sausages of all kinds as a snack food. Pork and veal join forces in the *Weisswürste* (white sausages), flavoured with pepper, parsley and onions. The establishments most observant of traditional standards never serve *Weisswürste* in the afternoon; they are then no longer considered fresh enough. *Bratwurst*, another sausage staple, is made of pork and grilled or sautéed. The best are the little ones from Nuremberg. You might also enjoy the spicy *Blutwurst* (blood sausage) or *Leberwurst* (liver sausage).

Also be on the look-out for a delicious snack with the misleading name of *Leberkäs*. Literally, this means 'liver-cheese', but it contains neither liver nor cheese, being rather a meatloaf of pork, bacon and beef, spiced with nutmeg, marjoram and onions, eaten hot or cold. Other great snacks include *Reiberdatschi*, or deep-fried potato pancakes; and *Obatzta*, a spicy mixture of creamy cheeses with chives, paprika, caraway seeds, salt and pepper, and thin slices of white radish *(Radi)*. Failing any of these, you will always be able to stimulate your thirst with giant salty pretzels *(Brez'n)*.

Desserts

Kaiserschmarrn is a thick pancake sliced in strips, sprinkled with raisins and powdered sugar and served with plum compote or apple sauce. *Dampfnudel* is a steamed dumpling swimming in custard. Other delicious treats offered in Bavaria are *Schwarzwälder Kirschtorte*, the cherry cake from the Black Forest, and *Apfelstrudel*; *Zwetschgendatschi* (plum cake) is very popular during the summer and autumn.

Beer

Bavarians endorse the old saying that there's good beer and better beer, but no bad beer. Especially not in Bavaria. Protected by the oldest food law, Duke William's purity law (*Reinheitsgebot*) of 1516, which forbids the use of anything but water, barley and hops in brewing, Bavarian beer is still made today from natural products without any chemical additives.

If you like beer dark with a slightly sweet, malty flavour, order a *Dunkles*. This is not served as cold as *Helles*, the more popular light lager brew. Refreshing and well worth a try is *Weissbier*, a light, slightly cloudy brew made from wheat instead of barley and left to ferment in the bottle. The measure for beer is the *Mass*, which is one litre; half of this is *eine Halbe*, the usual measure if you order a beer in a restaurant. In beer gardens, most beer is served in *Masskrüge* (litre glasses). *Weissbier* is usually served in half-litre measures,

⊘ SEASONAL DRINKING

It's not just at the Oktoberfest that the beer flows. In the third and fourth weeks before Easter, the so-called *Starkbierzeit* (Strong-beer Time), breweries promote their *Märzenbier* (March Ale). After Easter comes the *Maibockzeit*, when they push the strong, dark stuff. In the summer, everybody's thirsty enough not to need too much prompting.

though in beer gardens it can be mixed with lemonade *(Limo)*, served by the litre and called a *Russenmass*. Often the choice of cyclists who want to limit their alcohol intake, a *Radler* (cyclist) is a shandy made of *Helles* and *Limo*.

Wines

Southern Bavaria stopped making good wine some centuries ago, though the restaurants in Munich offer an excellent array of Rhine and Mosel wines, mostly white and usually made from the astonishingly versatile Riesling grape. The best dry Rhine Rieslings to look out for come from the red-soiled vineyards of villages such as Nierstein and Nackenheim. Also popular and widely available in and around Munich are wines from the Franconia region, especially around Würzburg. Here Silvaner as well as Riesling grapes produce excellent dry whites, usually bottled in the distinctive green *bocksbeutel*. Excellent whites and reds from Baden will also be found on most wine lists.

Weissbier, pretzel and Obatzta cheese

Other drinks

If refreshment rather than intoxication is your goal, you'll find a wide assortment of fruit juices, the most common being *Johannisbeersaft* (red or black currant), *Apfelsaft* (apple), *Orangensaft* (orange) and *Traubensaft* (non-alcoholic grape).

EATING OUT

TO HELP YOU ORDER

Waiter/waitress, please! **Bedienung, bitte.**
Could I/we have a table? **Ich hätte/Wir hätten gerne einen Tisch.**
The bill, please. **zahlen, bitte.**
I would like ... **Ich möchte gerne ...**

beer **ein Bier**
bread **etwas Brot**
butter **etwas Butter**
cheese **Käse**
coffee **einen Kaffee**
cream **Sahne**
dessert **eine Nachspeise**
eggs **Eier**
fish **Fisch**
meat **Fleisch**
menu **die Karte**
milk **Milch**
mineral water **Mineralwasser**
mustard **etwas Senf**
pepper **Pfeffer**
potatoes **Kartoffeln**
salad **Salat**
salt **Salz**
soup **eine Suppe**
starter **eine Vorspeise**
tea **einen Tee**
wine **Wein**
vegetables **Gemüse**

... AND READ THE MENU

Apfel apple
Blaukraut red cabbage
Blumenkohl cauliflower
Braten roast (pork or beef)
Brat-kartoffeln roast potatoes
Geräuchertes smoked meat
Gurkensalat cucumber salad
Hähnchen chicken (whole or half)
Kartoffel-knödel potato dumpling
Kraut cabbage
Lamm lamb
Rindfleisch beef
Rippchen smoked pork chops
Schinken ham
Schweine-fleisch pork
Semmel-knödel bread dumpling
Wild game
Wurst sausage

PLACES TO EAT

This selection focuses largely on traditional Bavarian eateries. We have included some of the major beer halls and beer gardens as they are an important focal point of Munich life; they usually serve light meals, snacks, and regional specialities. The following symbols correspond to the price of a 3-course meal for two people, not including wine.

€€€€ over 100 euros
€€€ 75–100 euros
€€ 50–75 euros
€ below 50 euros

INNENSTADT

Alois Dallmayr €€–€€€ *Dienerstrasse 14-15, tel: (089) 213 5100*. Restaurant above the sumptuous delicatessen of the same name, serving superb French cuisine. Open Tue–Fri 7–11pm, Sat noon–1:30pm, 7–11pm; the café is open Mon–Sat 9.30am–7pm.

Altes Hackerhaus € *Sendlinger Strasse 14, tel: (089) 260 5026, www.hackerhaus.de*. A venerable old tavern serving typical Bavarian cuisine including calves' lung with bread dumplings and crispy roast pork knuckle with potato dumplings. Open daily 10am–midnight.

Augustiner Restaurant €€ *Neuhauser Strasse 27, tel: (089) 2318 3257, www.augustiner-restaurant.com*. This delightful old beer hall is a Munich favourite, serving Bavarian specialities in plentiful portions. There's an attractive little garden at the back complete with fountain. Open Mon–Sat 9am–midnight, Sun 10am–midnight.

Austernkeller €€€–€€€€ *Stollbergstrasse 11, tel: (089) 298 787, www.austernkeller.de*. Well established seafood restaurant with the freshest oysters in town and a variety of delicious seafood, plus some French meat and poultry specialities. Open Mon–Fri 11.30–1am, Sat–Sun 5pm–1am.

Bratwurst-Glöckl am Dom € *Frauenplatz 9, tel: (089) 291 9450,* www.bratwurst-gloeckl.de. Old tavern serving Bavarian specialities. Known particularly for its *Nürnberger Bratwurst* – and the Dürer prints on the wall. Open Mon–Sat 10–1am, Sun until 11pm.

Pageou €€€–€€€€ *Kardinal-Faulhaber-Strasse 10, tel: (089) 2423 1310,* www.pageou.de/de. A well established, light and airy restaurant in the Fünf Höfe shopping precinct run by gourmet guru Karl Ederer. Creative interpretations of a range of cuisines. Open Tue–Sat for lunch and dinner.

Fraunhofer € *Fraunhoferstrasse 9, tel: (089) 266 460,* www.fraunhoferwirtshaus.de. With its wood panelling, hunting trophies, chandeliers and huge windows, this long-established beer hall/restaurant looks like a film set for a 19th-century tavern scene – but it's real. Great Bavarian food with many vegetarian options available. Open daily 4.30pm–1am.

La Galleria €€€–€€€€ *Sparkassenstrasse 11, tel: (089) 297 995,* www.ristorante-galleria.de. Upmarket Italian restaurant with excellent service and exciting, innovative cuisine. Open daily for lunch and dinner.

Garden Restaurant €€€–€€€€ *Bayerischer Hof Hotel, Promenadeplatz 4, tel: (089) 212 0993.* Mainly Italian specialities served in style; in the garden and on the terrace of the exclusive Bayerischer Hof hotel. Open daily for lunch and dinner.

Haxnbauer €€ *Sparkassenstrasse 6/Am Platzl, tel: (089) 216 6540,* www.kuffler.de/de/haxnbauer.php. Old Bavarian tavern specialising in spit-roast meats and regional dishes. Reservations advisable. Open daily 11am–midnight.

Hofbräuhaus am Platzl € *Am Platzl 9, tel: (089) 290 136 100,* www.hofbraeuhaus.de. The mothership of all the world's beer halls, in traditional Bavarian oompah style, with live brass band music, waitresses dressed in traditional *dirndl*, lashings of beer and local fare. An unmissable Munich experience. Open daily 9am–11pm.

PLACES TO EAT

Hofer €€ *Burgstrasse 5, tel: (089) 2421 0444*, www.hofer-der-stadtwirt.de. One of the few Gothic houses left in Munich (it was once the home of the Town Clerk), with good traditional fare. In the summer, eating out in the garden is a pleasure experience. Open Mon–Sat 10am–midnight.

Literaturhaus Café und Brasserie Oskar Maria €–€€€ *Salvatorplatz 1, tel: (089) 2919 6029*, www.oskarmaria.com. One of Munich's top gathering places, with the café dedicated to the writer Oskar Maria Graf (1894–1967). The restaurant offers a range of varied and imaginative dishes. Open daily 10am till midnight, Sun until 7pm.

Palaiskeller €€ *Bayerischer Hof Hotel, Promenadeplatz 2–6, tel: (089) 212 0990*. Well-prepared Bavarian cuisine in this vaulted restaurant belonging to the Bayerischer Hof hotel, priced about the same as the beer halls and *Weinstuben* nearby. Savour the fresh pretzels from the hotel's own bakery. Open daily 11–1am.

Prince Myshkin € *Hackenstrasse 2; tel. (089) 265 596*, www.prinzmyshkin.com/de. Munich's best vegetarian restaurant is a spacious and elegant affair serving imaginative dishes ranging from Indian treats to a selection of pasta dishes and pizzas to 'classics' like the potato-zucchini-truffle gratin. Local and organic ingredients. Open daily 11am–12.30am.

Ratskeller €€ *Marienplatz 8, tel: (089) 219 9890*, www.ratskeller.com. Labyrinth of an underground restaurant situated in the cellar of the Neues Rathaus. You can eat in one of the large rooms with their vaulted ceilings, choose a more intimate booth or sit out in the romantic courtyard. Typically hearty Bavarian fare and 1 litre *Steins* of beer. Open daily 10am–midnight.

Schuhbecks Südtiroler Stuben €€€€ *Am Platzl 6–8, tel: (089) 216 6900*, www.schuhbeck.de/gastronomie/suedtiroler-stuben. Michelin-starred restaurant run by chef Alfons Schuhbeck, with inspired blends of Eastern and Western cuisine. Menu depends on local produce available. Open Mon–Sat for lunch and dinner.

Spatenhaus an der Oper €€–€€€ *Residenzstrasse 12, tel: (089) 290 7060, www.kuffler.de/de/spatenhaus.php.* A classic for a romantic dinner before or after visiting the opera (opposite) or one of the nearby theatres. Locals also love the cosy ground floor for morning snacks or lunches involving expertly prepared Bavarian fare; upstairs is a more formal, elegant affair for high-class dining. Open daily 9.30–12:30am.

Vinorant Alter Hof €€–€€€ *Alter Hof 3, tel: (089) 2424 3733, www.restaurant-alter-hof.de.* Excellent restaurant in the old royal palace complex serving refined versions of traditional Franconian (north Bavarian) recipes. The Hof Keller wine cellar specialises in Franconian wines and serves delicious finger foods. Open Mon 11:30am–11pm, Tue, Sat 11:30am–midnight, Wed–Fri 11:30–1am.

Weisses Bräuhaus € *Tal 7, tel: (089) 290 1380, www.schneider-brauhaus.de.* Rambling old Bavarian-style beer hall serving its own *Schneider Weissbier* (wheat beer), including the ultra-strong and dark Aventinus. Great Bavarian and Austrian cuisine. Open daily 8–12:30am.

Zum Alten Markt €€ *Dreifaltigkeitsplatz 3, tel: (089) 299 995, www.zumaltenmarkt.de.* Popular restaurant decorated in hunting-lodge style. The grilled meats and salads are particularly good. Open Mon–Sat 11:30am–midnight.

Zum Spöckmeier €€ *Rosenstrasse 9, tel: (089) 268 088, www.spoeckmeier.com/gastronomie-muenchen.* This atmospheric Bavarian restaurant in the heart of Munich has been on the go since 1450. If you're there before noon, try the homemade *Weisswurst*, but you can drop in any time of day or night (Thursday to Saturday) as food is served until the early hours. Open Sun–Wed 9–1am, Thur–Sat to 3am.

THE STATION AND THE WEST

Augustiner Bräustuben € *Landsberger Strasse 19, tel: (089) 507 047, www.braeustuben.de.* Possibly the city centre's most authentic beer hall adjoining the Augustiner brewery. Superb Bavarian food and understandably popular with locals and brewery workers. Open daily 10am–midnight.

PLACES TO EAT

Chopan € *Elvirastrasse 18A, tel: (089) 1895 6459*, www.chopan.de. Munich has a large Afghan community whose restaurants provide a chance to sample the little known cuisine of that country. A few streets northwest of the Hauptbahnhof, Chopan is the pick of the bunch with tasty lamb and rice dishes but no alcohol. Open daily 6pm–midnight.

Hirschgarten € *Hirschgartenalle 1, tel: (089) 1799 9119*, www.hirschgarten.com. Munich's largest beer garden under wonderful mature chestnut trees in the western district of Laim, not far from Schloss Nymphenburg. There's seating for 8,000 and an adjoining game enclosure. Open daily 10am–midnight.

Löwenbräu-Keller € *Nymphenburgerstrasse 2, tel: (089) 526 021*, www.loewenbraeukeller.com/en. Traditional Munich beer hall just west of the city centre, close to the museums. Open daily 10am–midnight.

Schlosscafé im Palmenhaus €€ *Schlosspark Nymphenburg, tel: (089) 175 309*, www.palmenhaus.de/en. Romantic ambiance outside on the terrace as well as inside the big old glasshouse. Open Tue–Sat 10am–6pm.

Taxisgarten € *Taxis Strasse 12, tel: (089) 156 827*, www.taxisgarten.de. Small but very popular beer garden in the western district of Neuhausen/Gern. Open daily 11:30am–11pm.

ISAR AND THE EAST

Centro Espagñol €€ *Daiserstrasse 20, tel: (089) 763 653*, www.centroespanol.de. Small but long-established Spanish restaurant in the Sendling district, serving authentic Spanish cuisine. A variety of seafood, plus chicken and rabbit dishes and mouth-watering paella. Open Mon-Fri 5pm–1am, Sat until midnight.

Dreigroschenkeller € *Lilienstrasse 2, tel: (089) 3795 5834*, www.protutti.com/firmen/M/Dreigroschenkeller. Characterful cellar restaurant with a Threepenny Opera theme and an internationally-flavoured menu, located beneath the excellent Museum Lichtspiele cinema near the Deutsches Museum. Open Mon–Thur 5pm–1am, Fri and Sat to 3am.

Hofbräukeller €–€€ *Innere Wiener Strasse 19, tel: (089) 459 9250.* Not to be confused with the Hofbräuhaus, this is a popular venue for beer garden connoisseurs in the heart of Haidhausen. Open daily 10am–10pm.

Käfer-Schänke €€€€ *Prinzregentenstrasse 73, tel: (089) 416 8247, www.feinkost-kaefer.de/schaenke.* Fine but casual dining in chalet-style surroundings on the upper floor of Gerd Käfer's gourmet department store near the Villa Stuck in Bogenhausen. Dishes inspired from around the world. Open Mon–Sat 11.30am–11pm.

Muffatwerk € *Zellstrasse 4, tel: (089) 4587 5010, www.muffatwerk.de/en.* Located near the Müller'sches Volksbad, this beer garden, cafe and cultural venue is the place to head for a bit of alternative music, theatre and spoken word over a *Stein* or two of local suds. Open daily midday till late.

Rue des Halles €€€–€€€€ *Steinstrasse 18, tel: (089) 485 675, www.ruedeshalles.de.* A bistro-type restaurant in Haidhausen serving good quality French food, with traditional recipes rather than new culinary creations dominating the menu. Open daily 6pm–1am, warm dishes served till 11pm.

Zum Flaucher € *Isarauen 8, tel: (089) 7232 677, www.zumflaucher.de.* South of the centre right next to the river, this is one of Munich's best beer gardens, popular among cyclists, walkers and bathers. Open daily 10am–11midnight; restaurant only Thur–Sun.

SCHWABING AND THE NORTH

Chinesischer Turm € *Englischer Garten 3, tel: (089) 383 8730, www.chinaturm.de.* One of Munich's first and largest beer gardens, in the heart of the Englischer Garten. Guests can enjoy their drinks and typical Bavarian fare to accompaniments from the live Bavarian band on the tower. 7,000 seats. Open daily 7:30am–7:30pm.

Halali €€€ *Schönfeldstrasse 22, tel: (089) 285 909, www.restaurant-halali.de/uk.* Traditional Munich restaurant in a baronial setting serving Bavarian dishes and also imaginative new German cuisine using local ingredients. Good service. Reservations recommended. Open Mon–Fri for lunch and dinner, Sat dinner only.

La Villa im Bamberger Haus €€–€€€ *Brunnerstrasse 2, tel: (089) 308 8966, www.bambergerhaus.com.* Restaurant with lovely terrace in an 18th-century baroque villa in Luitpold Park (northwest of Schwabing). Bavarian food as well as Latin American dishes. Open Tue-Fri 5pm–1am, Sat–Sun 11–1am.

Max-Emanuel-Brauerei € *Adalbertstrasse 33, tel: (089) 271 5158, www.max-emanuel-brauerei.de/en.* Beer garden and tavern in the heart of Schwabing serving typical Bavarian fare. There is live music and lively atmosphere in the hall, which is also the place to come and dance rock´n roll, salsa and the tango. From April until October open daily 10:30am–midnight, beer garden to 10:30pm; from November until March open daily 5pm–midnight, beer garden closed.

Osterwaldgarten €€ *Keferstrasse 12, tel: (089) 3840 5040, www.osterwaldgarten.de.* A traditional restaurant and beer garden on the edge of the Englischer Garten, surrounded by ancient chestnut trees. Good food and excellent beer. Open daily 10am–1am, garden until 11pm.

Tantris €€€€ *Johann-Fichte-Strasse 7, tel: (089) 361 9590, www.tantris.de/en.* Superb continental cuisine prepared by one of Germany's top chefs and served in a modern restaurant with stark and startling décor. Outdoor dining. Open Tue–Sat for lunch and dinner. Reservations essential.

Zum Aumeister € *Sondermeierstrasse 9, tel: (089) 1893 1420, www.aumeister.de/en/willkommen.* Favourite excursion destination on the northern edge of the English Garden, best reached by bike. 2,500 seats in the beer garden. Cosy restaurant. Open Tue–Sat 11am–11pm, Sun till 6pm, in summer also Mon.

A–Z TRAVEL TIPS

A SUMMARY OF PRACTICAL INFORMATION

- **A** Accommodation 115
  - Airport 115
- **B** Bicycle hire 116
  - Budgeting for your trip 116
- **C** Camping 117
  - Car hire 118
  - Climate 118
  - Clothing 119
  - Crime and safety 119
- **D** Disabled travellers 119
  - Driving 120
- **E** Electricity 121
  - Embassies and consulates 121
  - Emergencies 122
- **G** Gay and lesbian travellers 122
  - Getting there 122
  - Guides and tours 123
- **H** Health and medical care 123
- **L** Language 124
- **M** Media 124
  - Money 125
- **O** Opening times 126
- **P** Police 126
  - Post offices 126
  - Public holidays 127
- **T** Telephone 127
  - Time zones 127
  - Tipping 128
  - Toilets 128
  - Tourist information 128
  - Transport 129
- **V** Visas and entry requirements 130
- **W** Websites and internet access 130
- **Y** Youth hostels 131

A

ACCOMMODATION (See also Camping, Youth hostels and the list of Recommended hotels starting on page 132)

The Munich Tourist Office (www.muenchen.de) publishes a free multilingual list of accommodation in the city, with full details of amenities and prices, available both online and from its offices in the city at Marienplatz and Hauptbahnhof. For the very best rates in Bavaria book online at www.hrs.com and www.booking.com.

In addition to hotels, there are inns *(Gasthof)* and B&Bs *(Pension)*. The Tourist Office can arrange for accommodation in private homes. If you are touring Bavaria by car, look for *'Zimmer frei'* (room to rent) signs. A list of hotels and inns in Upper Bavaria is available from Tourismusverband München-Oberbayern e.V., Radolfzeller Strasse 15, 81243 München, tel: (089) 8292 180, www.oberbayern.de.

Be aware that, in addition to the Oktoberfest, Munich hosts a variety of trade fairs and other events throughout the year, and so it's wise to check on dates with the tourist office and book rooms as far in advance as possible.

> I'd like a single/double room **Ich möchte bitte ein Einzel-/Doppelzimmer.**
> with bath/shower **mit Bad/Dusche**
> What's the rate per night? **Wieviel kostet es pro Nacht?**

AIRPORT (see also Transport)

Munich Airport (MUC): tel: (089) 97500, www.munich-airport.de.
Getting into Munich. Munich Airport is 30km (18 miles) east of the city centre. Suburban trains (S-Bahn) shuttle between the airport and the main railway station (Hauptbahnhof). The S-Bahn S8 runs every 20 minutes between the airport and Pasing via the city centre; the S1

service approaches the city centre from the direction of Laim in the west, also every 20 minutes. Both stop at stations on the way. If you're getting off at Ostbahnhof or Marienplatz it's quicker to take the S8; for points west of Hauptbahnhof the S1 is the best option. Both services take about 40 minutes to reach Hauptbahnhof, and the journey costs €11.20 for a single ticket. A taxi takes around the same time but costs around €50.

> Where can I get a taxi? **Wo finde ich ein Taxi?**
> How much is it to the centre? **Wieviel kostet es ins Zentrum?**

B

BICYCLE HIRE
With some 1,200km (800 miles) of cycle paths and its relatively flat terrain, Munich is renowned for being a cyclist's city. Most roads have special cycle lanes, but as well as getting you around town a bike is great for exploring the banks of the River Isar and the Englischer Garten. Information on tours can be obtained from Tourist Information or Mike's Bike Tours Munich, tel: (089) 2554 3987, www.mikesbiketours.com, which also handles bike hire. Radius Bikes (at the main station opposite platform 32, tel: (089) 54 34 87 77 40, www.radiustours.com) also rents out bikes between April and October.

BUDGETING FOR YOUR TRIP
Money saving tips:
Transport. MVV day tickets valid on all forms of city transport are a good deal if you are planning on making several journeys within 24 hours. A ticket for the entire network, including the airport, costs €12.80, for the city centre €6.60.

Museums. Entry to Munich's attractions ranges from €3 to €10, with the main museums charging around €7. Most of the museums in the Museum Quarter and some outside it charge a symbolic €1 admission on Sundays. Ask about family tickets if travelling with children.

CityTourCard. This discount card is available from the city transport (MVG) sales points and ticket machines, selected hotels and station kiosks (www.citytourcard-muenchen.com), and allows unlimited travel on all public transport and offers discounts of up to 20 percent on entry to 60 city attractions. It costs €10.90 a day or €20.90 for three days for the single adult inner area version and is well worth it.

Accommodation. Double room per night: luxury €250–400, mid-range €100–250, budget €50–100, hostel bed €25.

Meals. Three-course meal in a mid-range restaurant, around €35.

Drinks. Half-litre of beer €3.50, coffee €2–3, bottle of wine from €10.

C

CAMPING

Four major campsites are situated within the city limits:

Langwieder See, Eschenrieder Strasse 119, 81249 Munich, tel: (089) 864 1566, www.camping-langwieder-see.de. Campsite idyllically located next to the lake of the same name, northwest of Munich along the Augsburg–Stuttgart motorway. Open all year.

München–Obermenzing, Lochhausener Strasse 59, 81247 Munich, tel: (089) 811 2235, www.campingplatz-muenchen.de. Campsite to the northwest of Munich at Obermenzing (off the Augsburg-Stuttgart motorway). Open mid-March to end of October.

Campingplatz München-Thalkirchen, Zentralländstrasse 49, 81379 Munich, tel: (089) 723 1707, www.campingplatz-thalkirchen.de. Pleasantly situated campsite on the River Isar (the opposite bank to the zoo), with easy access to the city centre with the U-Bahn or No. 135 bus. Open mid-March to end of October.

The Tent (International Youthcamp Kapuzinerhölzl), In den Kirschen 30,

80992 Munich, tel: (089) 141 4300, www.the-tent.com. A campsite for young people in a park near the Botanical Garden (reached by tram No. 17 from Hauptbahnhof). A tent large enough to accommodate 300 people is also available. Open June to early October.

CAR HIRE (see also Driving)

Unless you intend to visit very remote places in the Alps, Bavaria's public transport network makes renting a car a luxury you can afford to forego. If you do decide to rent a car you'll need to have held a valid driver's licence for at least half a year; the minimum age is 19. If you do not pay by credit card you may have to pay a substantial cash deposit. Expect to pay from €35 per day for a medium-sized car if you haven't booked in advance online.

Sixt, www.sixt.com, tel: 1805-262 525
Europcar, www.europcar.com, tel: (089) 973 5020
Hertz, www.hertz.de, tel: (089) 978 8612
Avis, www.avis.com, tel: (089) 9759 7600
Enterprise, www.enterprise.de, tel: (089) 9788 0410

I'd like to rent a car **Ich möchte bitte ein Auto mieten.**
tomorrow **für morgen**
for one day/week **für einen Tag/für eine Woche**
Please include full insurance. **Bitte schliessen Sie eine Vollkaskoversicherung ab.**

CLIMATE

Munich's climate can go to extremes, from the bitterest cold in winter to hot and either dry or muggy in summer. The dry, warm wind from the south, known as *Föhn*, can result in very clear, hot, dry conditions wonderful for visitors. Munich's average temperatures are given below.

	J	F	M	A	M	J	J	A	S	O	N	D
Daytime °C	1	3	9	14	18	21	23	23	20	13	7	2
Daytime °F	34	37	48	57	64	70	73	73	68	55	45	35

CLOTHING

In winter you'll need a heavy coat and warm layers underneath. In summer you should bring plenty of lightweight garments, and a light wrap can come in handy for cool summer evenings. It may rain in spring and summer, so be prepared with a raincoat or umbrella.

CRIME AND SAFETY

Compared to many urban centres, Munich's crime rate is quite low. Nonetheless it's advisable to take all the normal precautions. Don't leave money or valuables in your car or hotel room; lock them in the hotel safe instead. If you are robbed, report the incident to the hotel receptionist and the nearest police station. The police will provide you with a certificate to present to your insurance company, or to your consulate if your passport has been stolen.

> I want to report a theft. **Ich möchte einen Diebstahl melden.**
> My handbag/wallet/passport has been stolen. **Meine Handtasche/Brieftasche/mein Pass ist gestohlen worden.**

D

DISABLED TRAVELLERS

City tours operated by Weisser Stadtvogel (www.stadtvogel.de) are suitable for visitors with disabilities.

DRIVING

To bring your car into Germany you will need: a national (or international for those coming from the US, Australia, or South Africa) driver's licence; car registration papers; a national identity car sticker; a red warning triangle in case of breakdown; and a first-aid kit.

Insurance. Third-party insurance is compulsory. For EU visitors, the international insurance certificate (Green Card) is no longer compulsory.

Low emission sticker. Driving inside Munich's Mittlere Ring (ring road) requires a low-emission sticker to be displayed prominently in the car windscreen (available online at www.umwelt-plakette.de).

Driving regulations. Drive on the right, pass on the left. When driving on the *Autobahn* (motorway, expressway), passing another vehicle on the right is strictly prohibited. In the absence of traffic lights, or stop or give-way signs, vehicles coming from the right have priority at intersections, unless otherwise indicated. At roundabouts (traffic circles), approaching cars must always give way to traffic that is already in the circle, unless otherwise indicated. Trams must be passed on the right and never at a stop (unless there's a traffic island).

> Driving Licence **Führerschein**
> Car Registration Papers **Kraftfahrzeugpapiere**

Speed limits. The speed limit is 100 km/h (62 mph) on all open roads except for motorways and divided highways, where there's no limit unless otherwise indicated (the suggested maximum speed is 130 km/h, or 81 mph). In town, the limit is 50 km/h (31 mph), except on the Mittlerer Ring, the six-lane ring road system around the city, where the limit is 60km/h (37mph).

Breakdowns. In the event of a breakdown on the Autobahn and other important roads, use one of the emergency telephones located every second kilometre (the direction of the nearest one is indicated by

> **Einbahnstrasse** One-way street
> **Einordnen** Get into lane
> **Fussgänger** Pedestrians
> **Kurzparkzone** Short-term parking
> **Links fahren** Keep left
> **Parken verboten** No parking
> **Umleitung** Detour
> **Vorsicht** Caution

a small arrow on the reflector poles at the roadside). Ask for Strassenwacht, run jointly by the two German automobile clubs ADAC and AVD. Assistance is free; towing and spare parts have to be paid for. For round-the-clock breakdown service, call (0180) 222 2222.

> Where's the nearest car park? **Wo ist der nächste Parkplatz?**
> Full tank, please. **Bitte volltanken.**
> Super/lead-free/diesel **Super/bleifreies Benzin/Diesel**
> I've had a breakdown. **Ich habe eine Panne.**
> There's been an accident. **Es ist ein Unfall passiert.**

E

ELECTRICITY
Germany has 220-volt, 50-cycle AC. Plugs are the standard Continental type for which British and North American appliances need an adaptor.

EMBASSIES AND CONSULATES
Canada: Tal 29, tel: (089) 219 9570.
Ireland: Denninger Strasse 15, tel: (089) 2080 5990.

South Africa: Sendlinger-Tor-Platz 5, tel: (089) 231 1630.
UK: Möhlstrasse 5, tel: (089) 211090.
US: Königinstrasse 5, tel: (089) 28880

EMERGENCIES
Emergency telephone numbers:
Police: 112 or 110
Fire and emergency medical services: 112

> I need a doctor **Ich brauche einen Arzt**
> an ambulance **einen Krankenwagen**
> a hospital **ein Krankenhaus**

G

GAY AND LESBIAN TRAVELLERS
Munich has an open atmosphere and is very accepting of all lifestyles. In particular, there is an area around the theatre district called Gärtnerplatz where there are many gay restaurants and clubs. The official tourist office website (www.muenchen.de) has a Gay Munich section.

GETTING THERE
By air. Munich Airport is a major hub receiving many European and intercontinental flights a day. However, the main airport for transatlantic flights is still Frankfurt, from where there are several flights a day to Munich. Average travel time from London to Munich is 1.5 hours, from New York 9 hours. BA (www.britishairways.com), easyJet (www.easyjet.com), Monarch (www.monarch.co.uk) and Lufthansa (www.lufthansa.com) all link Munich with London (all airports except City), Birmingham, Leeds/Bradford, Edinburgh and Manchester.

By coach. Eurolines (www.eurolines.co.uk) run coaches four times a week between London and Munich. The trip takes approximately 24 hours.

By rail. It's now easy to travel from London to Munich by train in a day. Eurostar links London with Brussels in just 2.5 hours, then high-speed Thalys trains link Brussels with Cologne in just 2.5 hours more. Change in Cologne for the ICE connection to Munich. Or you can travel overnight from London to Munich with just one change – simply take an evening Eurostar from London to Paris or Brussels then an overnight sleeping-car or couchette from Paris to Munich. Reservations are obligatory on all services.

GUIDES AND TOURS

City sightseeing tours by bus start from opposite the main entrance of the central railway station, in front of the Hertie department store. Enquire at Münchner Stadtrundfahrten www.stadtrundfahrten-muenchen.de. There are various tours available (hop-on-hop-off system), taking in city centre sights as well as peripheral attractions such as the Olympiapark, Schloss Nymphenburg and the Bavaria Filmstadt.

Cycle tours of the city are also available, and walking tours. Stattreisen München (www.stattreisen-muenchen.de), Weisser Stadtvogel (www.stadtvogel.de) and Radius Tours (www.radiustours.com) all offer special theme tours of the city.

H

HEALTH AND MEDICAL CARE

Citizens of European Union countries are eligible for free medical treatment and should obtain the European Health Insurance Card (EHIC) prior to their departure. However, it is still advisable to take out holiday insurance; a reputable policy will provide far more comprehensive coverage in the case of serious illness or accident.

Pharmacies are open during normal shopping hours. At night, on Sundays and on public holidays, all pharmacies display the address of the nearest pharmacy that is open. International pharmacies are located close to the main train station: Inter Apotheke, Elisenstrasse 5, tel: (089) 595 444, www.inter-apotheke.de; Schützenapotheke, Schützenstrasse 5, tel: (089) 557 661, www.schuetzenapotheke-muenchen.de.

Bavarian tap water is perfectly safe to drink; only rarely will you see the sign 'Kein Trinkwasser' (which means 'not drinking water', usually at public squares and on trains).

> Where's the nearest (all-night) pharmacy? **Wo ist die nächste Apotheke (mit Nachtdienst)?**

L

LANGUAGE

About one-third of the Munich population speaks a form of Bavarian dialect. Real Bavarian is difficult to understand, even for the many northern Germans who live in Munich, but Bavarians can often be persuaded to speak something closer to standard German. English is widely understood and spoken, and most of the larger shops have English-speaking staff, but don't take it for granted. Showing a willingness to use simple Bavarian or German phrases will go a long way.

> Do you speak English? **Sprechen Sie Englisch?**

M

MEDIA

Newspapers and magazines. Major British, American and Continental newspapers and magazines are on sale at newsstands in the city centre, as well as at larger hotels, the main railway station and the airport. The former English-language magazine *Munich Found* is no longer published in print, but the online version (www.munichfound.com) has valuable tips on culture and entertainment, and much else besides. The main local German-language newspapers are the heavyweight *Süddeutsche Zeitung* and the tabloid *TZ*.

MONEY

Currency. Germany's monetary unit is the euro (€), which is divided into 100 cents. Coins: 1, 2, 5, 10, 20 and 50 cents, and €1 and 2. Notes: €5, 10, 20, 50, 100, 200 and 500.

Banks and currency exchange. Foreign currency can be changed at ordinary banks *(Bank)*, savings banks *(Sparkasse)* and currency exchange offices *(Wechselstube)*. It can also be changed at hotels, travel agencies and Munich's central post office, but rates are not as good. Money can be changed at the ReiseBank in the main railway station from 7am to 10pm every day, or at the main post office. Always take your passport with you to change money or travellers' cheques.

Can I pay with this credit card? **Kann ich mit dieser Kreditkarte bezahlen?**
I want to change some pounds/dollars. **Ich möchte Pfund/Dollar wechseln.**
Can you cash a traveller's cheque? **Können Sie einen Reisescheck einlösen?**
Where's the nearest bank/currency exchange office? **Wo ist die nächste Bank/Wechselstube?**
Is there a cash machine near here? **Gibt es hier einen Geldautomaten?**
How much is that? **Wieviel kostet das?**

O

OPENING TIMES

Banks are usually open from 8.30am–12.30pm and 1.30–3.30 or 4pm, Monday to Friday (Thursday until 5.30pm). Some bigger banks in the city centre remain open during lunch hour. Banks at the airport operate daily from about 7am until around 9pm. Transactions can also be made at the central railway station daily from 6am–11pm.

Museum hours vary, but are usually from 9.30am–5pm or 6pm. Most museums have one late closing day and close on Mondays.

Shops are generally open from 9 or 10am–8pm, Monday to Friday, and till 4pm (some till 12.30pm) on Saturdays. Shops that are outside the main shopping areas in Munich usually close between 1 and 3pm.

P

POLICE

The police emergency number is **110**; Munich's central police station (Polizeipräsidium) is located at Ettstrasse 2, close to the Frauenkirche.

> Where's the nearest police station? **Wo ist die nächste Polizeistation?**

POST OFFICES

Munich's central post office is opposite the main railway station (Hauptbahnhof). It is open Monday–Friday 7:30am–8pm, Saturday 9am–4pm. Most post offices are open from 9am–6 or 7pm Monday to Friday (till noon or 1pm on Saturdays). **Postboxes** are painted yellow with a black post-horn.

Stamps can be purchased at yellow vending machines near post-

PUBLIC HOLIDAYS

1 January **Neujahr** New Year's Day
6 January **Heilige Drei Könige** Epiphany
1 May **Tag der Arbeit** Labour Day
15 August **Mariä Himmelfahrt** Assumption Day
3 October **Nationalfeiertag** Reunification Day
1 November **Allerheiligen** All Saints' Day
25, 26 December **Weihnachten** Christmas
Movable dates:
Karfreitag Good Friday
Ostermontag Easter Monday
Christi Himmelfahrt Ascension Day
Pfingstmontag Whit Monday
Fronleichnam Corpus Christi

TELEPHONE

The dialling code for Germany is 49. The dialling code for Munich from outside the city is 089. For international calls from Munich, dial 00 before the country code (44 for UK, 1 for US), then the area code and number of your destination.

Roaming charges for calls and data in the European Union have been reduced to affordable levels, meaning you can use your own mobile phone as you do at home. However purchasing a local SIM card will save you money if you are staying in Germany for longer periods or intending to make a lot of calls.

TIME ZONES

Germany follows Central European Time (GMT + 1). In summer, the clock is put one hour ahead (GMT + 2):

New York	London	**Munich**	Jo'burg	Sydney	Auckland
6am	11am	**noon**	noon	8pm	10pm

TIPPING

You can easily spend a holiday in Bavaria without giving a single tip. Waiters, maids and others providing services don't expect tips, and service is normally included in the price at restaurants.

TOILETS

Toilets may be labelled with symbols of a man or a woman or the initials W. C. Otherwise *Herren* (Gentlemen) and *Damen* (Ladies) or a double zero (00) sign are indicated.

Where are the toilets? **Wo sind die Toiletten?**

TOURIST INFORMATION

The Munich Tourist Board (www.muenchen.de) maintains two Tourist Offices in the city, located at Hauptbahnhof (the main railway station), Bahnhofsplatz 2 (open Mon–Sat 9am–8pm, Sun 10am–6pm), and in the Town Hall, Marienplatz 2 (open Mon–Fri 9am–7pm, Sat 9am–4pm, Sun 10am–2pm).

For information about Bavaria, contact the Munich-Upper Bavaria Tourist Association: Tourismusverband München-Oberbayern, Balanstarsse 57, tel: (089) 63 895 879, www.oberbayern.de.

The German National Tourist Board (www.germany.travel/en/index.html) maintains offices in many countries throughout the world, including:

Canada: 480 University Avenue, Suite 1500, Toronto, Ontario M5G 1V2, tel: (416) 968-1685.

UK: P.O. Box 2695, London W1A 3TN, tel: 020-7317 0900.
US: 122 East 42nd Street, 20th Floor, Suite 2000, New York, NY 10168-0072, tel: (212) 661-7200.

TRANSPORT

Munich is served by a highly efficient network of buses, trams, U-Bahn (underground railway) and S-Bahn (suburban railway, all co-ordinated by the MVV (Munich Transport and Tariff Association, www.mvv-muenchen.de). The U- and S-Bahn serve the city centre, while the S-Bahn goes out to suburbs and the surrounding countryside.

All forms of public transport operate from about 5am to 1am daily, with special night services till around 4am. Free maps and travel information are available at the tourist offices. Your ticket is not checked as you get on, but random checks are carried out. Fines of €40 are automatic if you are not able to produce a valid ticket when asked.

Tickets, interchangeable between U-Bahn, S-Bahn, buses and trams, entitle you to free transfers for up to 3 hours in one zone, 4 hours in two and more zones, so long as you travel in the same direction. Buy your tickets from the big blue vending machines at U- and S-Bahn stations (or on buses and at tram stops, hotels, tobacconists, newsagents and stationers that display a white 'K'). Vending machines are marked

---

What's the fare to ... ? **Wieviel kostet es nach ...?**
Where is the nearest bus stop? **Wo ist die nächste Bushaltestelle?**
When's the next bus to ...? **Wann geht der nächste Bus nach ...?**
I want a ticket to ... **Ich will eine Fahrkarte nach ...**
single/return **einfache Karte/Rückfahrkarte**
Will you tell me when to get off? **Könnten Sie mir bitte sagen, wann ich aussteigen muss.**

Einzelfahrkarte (single ticket) or *Streifenkarte* (strip ticket). The strip tickets work out cheaper if you intend to make several trips. Be sure to cancel tickets in the blue cancelling machines positioned at platform entrances and in buses and trams; if you have a strip ticket you need to cancel two strips per zone travelled (persons aged 15-20 years cancel only one strip per zone, children one strip per trip), unless you travel only one stop by U- or S-Bahn or two stops by bus or tram – then one strip is sufficient.

VISAS AND ENTRY REQUIREMENTS

Germany is part of the Schengen area meaning there are no limitations on the amount of time EU citizens can spend there. Travellers from the US, Canada, Australia, New Zealand can stay visa-free for up to 90 days. South Africans need to apply for a Schengen visa.

WEBSITES AND INTERNET ACCESS

Most hotels now offer free or paid wi-fi to guests or at least a computer hooked up to the internet for guest use. As across Europe, internet cafés are more or less a thing of the past in Munich but one (Coffee Fellows: Schützenstrasse 14, open Mon–Thur 7am–10pm, Fri 7am–midnight, Sat 8am–midnight, Sun 8am–10pm) near the main railway station has managed to survive. Many cafés and restaurants also offer wi-fi though not as many as you might expect in such a major city.

Useful websites:

www.muenchen.de (Munich Tourist Board).
www.munichfound.com (practical information and cultural tips).
https://events.in-muenchen.de/region (website of *In-München* listings magazine).
www.deutsches-museum.de (Deutsches Museum site).

www.oktoberfest.de (most comprehensive Oktoberfest site available).
https://fcbayern.com/de (official site of Bayern Munich football club).

Y

YOUTH HOSTELS

If you're planning to make extensive use of youth hostels throughout your stay in Munich, it is a good idea to obtain an international membership card from your national youth hostel association. For full information about hostels in Munich and Germany as a whole, contact the German Youth Hostel Association (Deutsches Jugendherbergswerk– DJH, www.jugendherberge.de. All charge approximately €25 (plus €4 if you are over 27 years of age) for a dorm bed for a night and breakfast. The following youth hostels are located in and around Munich:

Jugendherberge Burg Schwaneck, Burgweg 10, 82049 Pullach im Isartal, tel: (089) 7448 6670, www.burgschwaneck.de. Located in a castle to the south of Munich, overlooking the picturesque Isar Valley.

Jugendherberge München-Park, Miesingstrasse 4, 81379 Munich, tel: (089) 7857 6770, www.muenchen-park.jugendherberge.de. Modern youth hostel in the southern district of Thalkirchen, by the river.

Jugendherberge München-Ciy, Wendl-Dietrich-Strasse 20, 80634 Munich, tel: (089) 2024 4490, www.muenchen-city.jugendherberge.de. Pleasant youth hostel in the district of Neuhausen.

In addition, Munich has many independent hostels with city centre locations. These do not require you to have a membership card.

RECOMMENDED HOTELS

The following selection of recommended hotels is arranged under headings according to geographical location: Innenstadt (for the Old City centre); the Station and the west (for the station and Oktoberfest); Isar and the east (for locations along or near the river and quick access to the trade fair grounds at Riem); Schwabing and the north (including spots near the Englischer Garten and Olympiapark).

There are hotel booking facilities at the main tourist information offices in Munich (see page 128). Do check weekend rates online – there might be a bargain. However, because Munich is an important conference and trade fair centre, it is important to book good and early; during the Oktoberfest, which lasts for 16 days up to the first Sunday in October, rooms should be reserved up to a year in advance; many stay outside Munich in places such as Augsburg and Nuremburg and commute in by train.

The symbols below are a guide to the price of a standard double room with bathroom. Breakfast is usually included. The so-called hotels 'garni' supply breakfast only, no restaurant meals. All prices are inclusive of service and tax.

€€€€ over 250 euros
€€€ 190–250 euros
€€ 100–190 euros
€ below 100 euros

INNENSTADT

Asam Stadthotel €€ *Josephspitalstrasse 3, 80331 Munich, tel: (089) 2309 700*, www.hotel-asam.de. Pleasant family-run hotel in a converted five-storey townhouse just five minutes' walk from Marienplatz. The large and airy rooms are luxuriously appointed and have beautiful granite bathrooms. Rear bedrooms look over pleasant gardens. 16 rooms, 8 suites.

INNENSTADT

Bayerischer Hof €€€€ *Promenadeplatz 2-6, 80333 Munich, tel: (089) 21200, www.bayerischerhof.de.* Luxury hotel in the heart of Munich built in 1841 on the orders of Ludwig I and now also occupying the neighbouring Palais Montgelas. You can take your pick from five different elegant styles of room, and facilities include bars and restaurants, rooftop garden, swimming pool, sauna and shops. 340 rooms.

Cortiina €€€ *Ledererstrasse 8, 80331 Munich, tel: (089) 2422 490, www.cortiina.com.* Generally regarded as one of the city centre's best places to get a good night's sleep, the chic retro-designed pads at this trendy hotel are superb places to kick back in style after a day's sightseeing.

Hotel An der Oper €€€ *Falkenturmstrasse 10, 80331 Munich, tel: (089) 2900 270, www.hotelanderoper.de.* Five-floor four-star hotel just off Maximilianstrasse. The 69 elegantly designed, comfortable rooms, the restaurant and superb location make this hotel a reasonably good deal.

Hotel Exquisit €€€ *Pettenkoferstrasse 3, 80336 Munich, tel: (089) 551 990, www.hotel-exquisit.net.* Comfortable hotel located close to Sendlinger Tor, a 10-minute walk from Marienplatz. Good buffet breakfast until 2pm at weekends. Sauna, solarium, garden terrace. 50 rooms.

Hotel Olympic €€-€€€ *Hans-Sachs-Strasse 4, 80469 Munich, tel: (089) 231 890, www.hotel-olympic.de.* Tastefully converted Victorian villa situated on a pretty street in the Glockenbach district between Gärtnerplatz and Sendlingertor. Most rooms look out onto a peaceful courtyard. Friendly service, excellent breakfast. 38 rooms.

H'Otello B'01 €€-€€€ *Baaderstrasse 1, 80469 Munich, tel: (089) 216 310, www.hotello.de/b01-muenchen.* Stylish hotel with modern interior, located in the fashionable Gärtnerplatz district, just five minutes' walk from Marienplatz. Great breakfast. 50 rooms.

Kempinski Hotel Vier Jahreszeiten München €€€€ *Maximilianstrasse 17, 80539 Munich, tel: (089) 2125 2799, www.kempinski.com/en/munich/hotel-vier-jahreszeiten.* This is Munich's most distinctive hotel, part of the fabric of elegant Maximilianstrasse. Its rooms and suites are sumptuously appointed, and the large bathrooms are equipped with all sorts of special treats. Facilities include a restaurant, bar, pool, sauna and solarium. 308 rooms and suites.

Mandarin Oriental €€€€ *Neuturmstrasse 1, 80331 Munich, tel: (089) 290 980*, www.mandarinoriental.com. A wedge-shaped neoclassical building around the corner from the Hofbräuhaus houses Munich's top hotel. It is known for having the most spacious rooms in the city, each one fitted out with hand-made furnishings. There's a rooftop terrace with heated swimming pool and spectacular 360 degree city views. The sweeping marble staircase in the lobby leads up to the acclaimed Mark's restaurant, a gourmet's delight. 53 rooms, 20 suites.

Platzl Hotel €€€ *Sparkassenstrasse 10, 80331 Munich, tel: (089) 237 030*, www.platzl.de. On the site of an old mill dating from the 16th century, the Platzl has tastefully appointed rooms, most in contemporary style but with the option of the 'Bavarian Suite'. The 'Moorish Kiosk' recreation area has state of the art fitness and wellness facilities. 167 rooms.

Schlicker 'Zum goldenen Löwen' €€ *Tal 8, 80331 Munich, tel: (089) 242 8870*, www.hotel-schlicker.de. You can't get more central than this comfortable hotel garni in a building dating back to the 16th century, just steps away from Marienplatz. Run by the same family for four generations. 68 rooms.

THE STATION AND THE WEST

Hotel Alfa München Zentrum €–€€ *Hirtenstrasse 22, 80335 Munich, tel: (089) 5459 530*, www.hotel-alfa.de. Cheap and cheerful hotel garni conveniently situated near the station, but in a quiet side-street location. Garage and other parking available. 76 rooms.

City Hotel €–€€€ *Schillerstrasse 3a, 80336 Munich, tel: (089) 515 5390*, www.city-hotel-muenchen.de. Six-storey hotel close to the station that combines cosiness with a modern if slightly bland design. All bedrooms are ensuite. Buffet breakfast. 71 rooms.

Cocoon €€ *Lindwurmstrasse 35, 80337 Munich, tel: (089) 5999 3907*, www.cocoon-hotels.de. For something a little funkier in the station area, go for this brightly-hued design hotel, all retro veneers and big panels of colour. Fully wired for the latest gadgets and with some quirky features such as in-room showers and virtual fireplaces. 46 rooms.

Deutsches Theater €–€€ *Schwanthalerstrasse 15, 80336 Munich, tel: (089) 889 9950*, www.hotel-deutsches-theater.com. Relaxed hotel garni in a central location. All rooms are decorated with Laura Ashley-style fabrics. Lobby bar open 24 hours a day; good breakfast buffet. 27 rooms.

Eden-Hotel-Wolff €€–€€€€ *Arnulfstrasse 4, 80335 Munich, tel: (089) 551 150*, www.eden-hotel-wolff.de. The plain exterior of this hotel opposite the station belies the class of the establishment, from the excellent service to the individual, modern decor of each room. Modern wellness centre including gym and sauna; conference facilities. 210 rooms and suites.

Europäischer Hof €–€€ *Bayerstrasse 31, 80335 Munich, tel: (089) 551 510*, www.heh.de. Big but homely, family-operated hotel opposite the Hauptbahnhof, with various classes of rooms available. Paintings in the rooms and corridors provide a personal touch. 149 rooms.

Hahn Hotel €€–€€€ *Landsberger Strasse 117, 80339 Munich, tel: (089) 5108 9590*, www.hotel-hahn.de. Family-run hotel garni decorated in the Bavarian rustic style, with friendly service. Parking and bar. 40 rooms.

InterCityHotel München €€ *Bayerstrasse 10, 80335 Munich, tel: (089) 444 440*, www.intercityhotel.com. This is Munich's original station hotel, once an Art Nouveau showpiece but now completely refashioned in contemporary style. Pleasant rooms all with en-suite; restaurant and bar. 198 rooms.

Laimer Hof €–€€ *Laimerstrasse 40, 80639 Munich, tel: (089) 178 0380*, https://laimerhof.de. Guests heap praise on Munich's best small family-run hotel near Schloss Nymphenburg. Occupying an elegant villa, rooms are cosy and comfortable but it's the enthusiastic staff and friendly service that make this place a firm favourite. 23 rooms.

RECOMMENDED HOTELS

Mariandl €–€€ *Goethestrasse 51, 80336 Munich, tel: (089) 552 9100, www.mariandl.com.* If it's character you're after, look no further than this neo-Gothic pile halfway between the Hauptbahnhof and the Oktoberfest grounds. Rooms are elegantly old-fashioned with high ceilings, parquet floors and crystal chandeliers. The on-site Café am Beethovenplatz is one of Munich's top jazz venues.

Mercure Hotel Muenchen City Center €€ *Senefelderstasse 9, 80336 Munich, tel: (089) 551 320, www.mercure.com.* Well located hotel just 300m from the station. Restaurant with regional and international cuisine, beer garden; conference rooms. 167 rooms.

Mirabell €€ *Landwehrstrasse 42 (entrance Goethestrasse), 80336 Munich, tel: (089) 549 1740, www.m-privathotels.de/mirabell.* Good value family-run hotel garni a couple of blocks from the main railway station offering 68 modern, immaculately kept business-standard rooms.

Nymphenburg €€ *Nymphenburger Strasse 141, 80636 Munich, tel: (089) 121 5970, www.hotel-nymphenburg.de.* Good service in this quiet hotel situated in the district of Neuhausen, not far from Schloss Nymphenburg. Pleasant, individually-designed rooms, most facing away from the street, some with balcony. 44 rooms.

Pension Westfalia € *Mozartstrasse 23, 80336 Munich, tel: (089) 530 337, www.pension-westfalia.de.* The closest beds to the Oktoberfest venue (though you'd be very lucky to bag a room here during the event), the rest of the year this simple bed and breakfast enjoys a quiet location. Some quaint touches.

Uhland Garni €€ *Uhlandstrasse 1, 80336 Munich, tel: (089) 543 350, www.hotel-uhland.de.* Family-run hotel garni in a Jugendstil villa adjacent to the Theresienwiese. A good choice for families as many units contain bunk beds for children. Continental and traditional Bavarian breakfast included. 27 rooms.

Wombats City Hostel € *Senefelderstrasse 1, 80336 Munich, tel: (089) 5998 9180, www.wombats-hostels.com.* Munich's best backpacker hostel with ample facilities, a happening vibe and a great location near the main railway station.

ISAR AND THE EAST

Admiral München €€ *Kohlstrasse 9, 80469 Munich, tel: (089) 216 350, www.hotel-admiral.de.* Hotel garni in a tranquil location on the west bank of the Isar near the Deutsches Museum, a short amble from the central city sights. Some of the elegantly furnished rooms have a balcony overlooking the lovely garden. Bar available. Excellent breakfast buffet. 33 rooms.

Hilton Munich City €€–€€€€ *Rosenheimer Strasse 15, 81667 Munich, tel: (089) 48040, www3.hilton.com.* In the district of Haidhausen near the Gasteig cultural centre, and just a short walk from the Isar and the Deutsches Museum. Facilities include two restaurants serving German and regional specialities, the Caffè Cino and a fully-equipped business centre. 480 rooms.

Holiday Inn Munich City Centre €€–€€€ *Hochstrasse 3, 81669 Munich, tel: (089) 48030, www.ihg.com.* Opposite the Gasteig cultural centre, above the Isar, this large hotel has elegant modern decor and all imaginable facilities, including swimming pool, sauna and steam bath. Business centre and extensive conference facilities. 582 rooms.

Hotel Domus €€ *St-Anna-Strasse 31, 80538 Munich, tel: (089) 217 7730, www.domus-hotel.de.* Modern five-storey hotel garni in the peaceful district of Lehel between Maximilianstrasse and the Englischer Garten, and close to the Isar. Tastefully furnished rooms in a contemporary style, all with bathrooms with shower-tub combinations. Excellent Italian restaurant, the Facile; good breakfast buffet. 45 rooms.

Leonardo Hotel München City West €€–€€€ *Brudermühlstrasse 33, 81371 Munich, tel: (089) 724 940, www.leonardo-hotels.com.* Modern hotel to the southwest of the centre close to the Isar and the Flaucher beer garden. All rooms equipped with a kitchen; also a fitness centre with sauna and solarium. Italian restaurant, bar and massive roof-deck with superb view. 98 rooms.

Prinzregent am Friedensengel €€–€€€ *Riemer Strasse 350, 81829 Munich, tel: (089) 217 683 115, www.prinzregent.de.* An exclusive hotel garni decorated in a fusion of Bavarian and Italian styles. Facilities include sauna, bar, chemin room, and beer garden. Breakfast can be enjoyed in the sheltered inner courtyard. 91 rooms, recently renovated.

Ritzi €€€ *Maria-Theresia-Strasse 2a, 81675 Munich, tel: (089) 414 240 890, www.hotel-ritzi.de.* Located on the eastern side of the Isar near the Maximilianeum, the Ritzi has character-filled rooms, all with an 'exotic lands' theme. Much-lauded restaurant.

Sheraton Munich Arabellapark €€€–€€€€ *Arabellastrasse 5, 81925 Munich, tel: (089) 92320, www.sheratonarabellapark.com.* A 22-storey building located in the Bogenhausen district of the city this is one of the largest hotels in Munich. It has a swimming pool on the top floor, plus a series of whirlpools, saunas and steam rooms. Conference facilities. 446 rooms.

SCHWABING AND THE NORTH

Four Points by Sheraton Munich Olympiapark €€€ *Helene-Mayer-Ring 12, 80809 Munich, tel: (089) 357 510, www.starwoodhotels.com.* Modern hotel located in the heart of the Olympic Village, just a short walk from the Olympiapark and so ideal for those who want to make use of the facilities there. Bavarian restaurant and bar; rooms among the most modern and best kept in the city. 105 rooms.

Gästehaus Englischer Garten €–€€ *Liebergesellstrasse 8, 80802 Munich, tel: (089) 3839 410, www.hotelenglischergarten.de.* Delightful old villa in a tranquil location by the Englischer Garten. Nicely furnished rooms, and garden at the rear where breakfast is served in the summer. Most rooms have ensuite bathrooms; apartments with kitchenettes in annexe. 25 rooms.

Haus International € *Elisabethstrasse 87, 80797 Munich, tel: (089) 120 060, www.haus-international.de.* In western Schwabing, this classic youth hostel has neither curfew nor age limit, and no youth hostel card is required. Restaurant, bar and disco. 546 beds in basic rooms.

SCHWABING AND THE NORTH

Hilton Munich Park Hotel €€€–€€€€ *Am Tucherpark 7, 80538 Munich, tel: (089) 38450, www3.hilton.com.* This 15-storey hotel in a quiet location adjacent to the Englischer Garten was created for the 1972 Olympic Games. Facilities include restaurant, bar, pool and fitness and beauty centre; fine views of the Alps in clear weather. 479 rooms.

Hotel Hauser €€ *Schellingstrasse 11, 80799 Munich, tel: (089) 286 6750, www.hotel-hauser.de.* Traditional, family-run hotel garni near the University and Englischer Garten, with sauna and solarium plus parking and free wi-fi. Welcomes children. 33 rooms.

Hotel-Pension Am Siegestor € *Akademiestrasse 5, 80799 Munich, tel: (089) 399 550, www.siegestor.com.* This friendly, family-run guesthouse is spread over the top three floors of a large townhouse opposite the Academy of Arts and just 100m from the Siegestor. Some rooms with en-suite bathrooms, some shared. The 20 rooms here are a great deal.

Innside Parkstadt Schwabing €€€ *Mies-van-der-Rohe-Strasse 10, 80807 Munich, tel: (089) 354 080, www.melia.com.* Situated in the north of Schwabing (close to the motorway A9 to Nuremberg and the Mittlere Ring) this hotel at the bottom of the HighLight Towers by Helmut Jahn offers a stunning modern ambiance and utmost comfort. 160 studios and suites.

La Maison €€€ *Occamstrasse 24, 80802 Munich, tel: (089) 3303 5550, www.hotel-la-maison.com.* Wonderfully stylish boutique design hotel in Altschwabing offering retro chic bedrooms in shades of grey, cream and black. Equally trendy bar downstairs and friendly service.

DICTIONARY

ENGLISH–GERMAN

adj adjective **adv** adverb **BE** British English **n** noun **prep** preposition **v** verb

A

accept v akzeptieren
access n der Zutritt
accident der Unfall
accommodation die Unterkunft
account n (bank) das Konto
acupuncture die Akupunktur
adapter der Adapter
address n die Adresse
admission (price) der Eintritt
after nach; **~noon** der Nachmittag; **~shave** das Aftershave
age n das Alter
agency die Agentur
AIDS AIDS
air n die Luft; **~ conditioning** die Klimaanlage; **~-dry** lufttrocknen; **~ pump** die Luftpumpe; **~line** die Fluggesellschaft; **~mail** die Luftpost; **~plane** das Flugzeug; **~port** der Flughafen
aisle der Gang; **~ seat** der Platz am Gang
allergic allergisch; **~ reaction** die allergische Reaktion
allow erlauben
alone allein
alter v umändern
alternate route die Alternativroute
aluminum foil die Aluminiumfolie
amazing erstaunlich
ambulance der Krankenwagen
American adj amerikanisch
amusement park der Vergnügungspark
anemic anämisch
anesthesia die Anästhesie
animal das Tier
ankle das Fußgelenk
antibiotic n das Antibiotikum
antiques store das Antiquitätengeschäft
antiseptic cream die antiseptische Creme
apartment das Apartment
appendix (body part) der Blinddarm
appetizer die Vorspeise
appointment der Termin
arcade die Spielhalle
area code die Ortsvorwahl
arm n (body part) der Arm
aromatherapy die Aromatherapie
around (the corner) um; **~ (price)** ungefähr
arrival Ankunft
arrive ankommen
artery die Arterie
arthritis die Arthritis
art die Kunst
Asian adj asiatisch
aspirin das Aspirin
asthmatic asthmatisch
ATM der Bankautomat; **~ card** die Bankkarte
attack v angreifen
attraction (place) die Sehenswürdigkeit
attractive attraktiv
Australia das Australien
Australian adj australisch
automatic automatisch; **~ car** das Auto mit Automatikschaltung
available verfügbar

B

baby das Baby; **~ bottle** die Babyflasche; **~ wipe** das Baby-Pflegetuch; **~sitter** der Babysitter
back (body part) der Rücken; **~ache** die Rückenschmerzen; **~pack** der Rucksack
bag die Tasche
baggage [BE] das Gepäck; **~ claim** die Gepäckausgabe; **~ ticket** der Gepäckschein
bake v backen
bakery die Bäckerei
ballet das Ballett
bandage das Pflaster
bank n die Bank
bar (place) die Bar
barbecue (device) n der Grill
barber der Herrenfriseur
baseball der Baseball
basket (grocery store) der Einkaufskorb
basketball der Basketball
bathroom das Bad
battery die Batterie
battleground das Schlachtfeld
be v sein
beach der Strand
beautiful wunderschön; **~** schön
bed n das Bett; **~ and breakfast** die Pension
before vor
begin beginnen
beginner der Anfänger
behind (direction) hinter

DICTIONARY

beige *adj* beige
belt der Gürtel
best *adj* beste;
 ~ before mindestens haltbar bis
better besser
bicycle das Fahrrad
big groß; **~ger** größer
bike route die Radroute
bikini der Bikini
bill *n* **(money)** der Geldschein; **~** *n* **(of sale)** die Rechnung
bird der Vogel
birthday der Geburtstag
black *adj* schwarz
bladder die Blase
bland fad
blanket die Decke
bleed bluten
blender der Mixer
blood das Blut; **~ pressure** der Blutdruck
blouse die Bluse
blue *adj* blau
board *v* einsteigen; **~ing pass** die Bordkarte
boat *n* das Boot
boil *v* kochen
bone *n* der Knochen
book *n* das Buch; **~store** der Buchladen
boot der Stiefel
boring langweilig
botanical garden der botanische Garten
bother *v* belästigen
bottle die Flasche; **~ opener** der Flaschenöffner
bowl *n* die Schüssel
boxing match der Boxkampf

boy der Junge; **~friend** der Freund
bra der BH
bracelet das Armband
brake (car) die Bremse
breaded paniert
break *v* **(bone)** brechen
breakdown (car) die Panne
breakfast *n* das Frühstück
break-in (burglary) *n* der Einbruch
breast die Brust; **~feed** *v* stillen
breathe atmen
bridge die Brücke
briefs (clothing) der Schlüpfer
bring bringen
British *adj* britisch
broken kaputt; **~ (bone)** gebrochen
brooch die Brosche
broom der Besen
brother der Bruder
brown *adj* braun
bug (insect) *n* das Insekt
building das Gebäude
burn *v* brennen
bus *n* der Bus; **~ station** der Busbahnhof; **~ stop** die Bushaltestelle; **~ ticket** die Busfahrkarte; **~ tour** die Busreise
business *adj* Geschäfts-; **~ card** die Visitenkarte; **~ center** das Geschäftszentrum; **~ class** die Business-Class; **~ hours** die Öffnungszeiten
butcher *n* der Fleischer

buttocks der Po
buy *v* kaufen
bye auf Wiedersehen

C

cabaret das Kabarett
cable car die Seilbahn
cafe (place) das Café
call *v* **(phone)** anrufen; **~** *n* der Anruf – **collect** ein R-Gespräch führen
calorie die Kalorie
camera die Kamera; **~ case** die Kameratasche; **digital ~** die Digitalkamera
camp *v* campen; **~ing stove** der Campingkocher; **~site** der Campingplatz
can opener der Dosenöffner
Canada das Kanada
Canadian *adj* kanadisch
cancel stornieren
candy die Süßigkeit
canned good die Konserve
canyon der Canyon
car das Auto; **~ hire [BE]** die Autovermietung; **~ park [BE]** der Parkplatz; **~ rental** die Autovermietung; **~ seat** der Autositz
carafe die Karaffe
card *n* die Karte; **ATM ~** die Bankkarte; **credit ~** die Kreditkarte; **debit ~** die EC-Karte; **phone ~** die Telefonkarte
carry-on *n* **(piece of hand luggage)** das Handgepäckstück

cart (grocery store) der Einkaufswagen; **~ (luggage)** der Gepäckwagen
carton (of cigarettes) die Stange (Zigaretten); **~ (of groceries)** die Packung
cash *n* das Bargeld; **~** *v* einlösen
cashier der Kassierer
casino das Casino
castle das Schloss
cathedral die Kathedrale
cave *n* die Höhle
CD die CD
cell phone das Handy
Celsius Celsius
centimeter der Zentimeter
certificate das Zertifikat
chair *n* der Stuhl; **~ lift** der Sessellift
change *v* **(baby)** wickeln; **~ (buses)** umsteigen; **~ (money)** wechseln; **~** *n* **(money)** das Wechselgeld
charge *v* **(credit card)** belasten; **~ (cost)** verlangen
cheap billig; **~er** billiger
check *v* **(luggage)** aufgeben; **~ (on something)** prüfen; *n* **(payment)** der Scheck; **~-in** das Check-in; **~ing account** das Girokonto; **~-out** das Check-out
Cheers! Prost!

chemical toilet die Campingtoilette
chemist [BE] die Apotheke
chest (body part) die Brust; **~ pain** die Brustschmerzen
chewing gum der Kaugummi
child das Kind; **~'s seat** der Kinderstuhl
children's menu das Kindermenü
children's portion die Kinderportion
Chinese adj chinesisch
chopsticks die Stäbchen
church die Kirche
cigar die Zigarre
cigarette die Zigarette
class n die Klasse; **business ~** die Business-Class; **economy ~** die Economy-Class; **first ~** die erste Klasse
classical music die klassische Musik
clean v reinigen; ~ adj (clothes) sauber; **~ing product** das Reinigungsmittel
clear v (on an ATM) löschen
cliff die Klippe
cling film [BE] die Klarsichtfolie
close v (a shop) schließen
closed geschlossen
clothing die Bekleidung; **~ store** das Bekleidungsgeschäft
club n der Club

coat der Mantel
coin die Münze
colander das Sieb
cold n (sickness) die Erkältung; ~ adj (temperature) kalt
colleague der Kollege
cologne das Kölnischwasser
color n die Farbe
comb n der Kamm
come v kommen
complaint die Beschwerde
computer der Computer
concert das Konzert; **~ hall** die Konzerthalle
condition (medical) die Beschwerden
conditioner (hair) die Spülung
condom das Kondom
conference die Konferenz
confirm bestätigen
congestion (medical) der Blutstau
connect (internet) verbinden
connection (travel/internet) die Verbindung; **~ flight** der Anschlussflug
constipated verstopft
consulate das Konsulat
consultant der Berater
contact v kontaktieren
contact lens die Kontaktlinse; **~ solution** Kontaktlinsenlösung
contagious ansteckend
convention hall der Kongresssaal
conveyor belt das Förderband

cook v kochen
cool adj (temperature) kalt
copper n das Kupfer
corkscrew der Korkenzieher
cost v kosten
cotton die Baumwolle
cough v husten; **~** n der Husten
country code die Landesvorwahl
cover charge der Preis pro Gedeck
cream (ointment) die Creme
credit card die Kreditkarte
crew neck der runde Halsausschnitt
crib das Kinderbett
crystal n (glass) das Kristall
cup n die Tasse
currency die Währung; **~ exchange** der Währungsumtausch; **~ exchange office** die Wechselstube
current account [BE] das Girokonto
customs der Zoll
cut v schneiden; **~** n (injury) der Schnitt
cute süß
cycling das Radfahren

D
damage v beschädigen
dance v tanzen; **~ club** der Tanzclub; **~ing** das Tanzen
dangerous gefährlich
dark adj dunkel

date n (calendar) das Datum
day der Tag
deaf adj taub
debit card die EC-Karte
deck chair der Liegestuhl
declare v (customs) deklarieren
decline v (credit card) ablehnen
deep adj tief
degree (temperature) das Grad
delay v verzögern
delete v (computer) löschen
delicatessen das Feinkostgeschäft
delicious lecker
denim das Denim
dentist der Zahnarzt
denture die Zahnprothese
deodorant das Deodorant
department store das Kaufhaus
departure (plane) der Abflug
deposit v (money) einzahlen; **~** n (bank) die Einzahlung
desert n die Wüste
detergent das Waschmittel
develop v (film) entwickeln
diabetic adj diabetisch; **~** n der Diabetiker
dial v wählen
diamond der Diamant
diaper die Windel
diarrhea der Durchfall
diesel der Diesel

DICTIONARY

difficult schwierig
digital digital;
~ **camera** die Digitalkamera; ~ **photo** das Digitalfoto; ~ **print** der digitale Ausdruck
dining room das Esszimmer
dinner das Abendessen
direction die Richtung
dirty schmutzig
disabled adj (person) behindert; ~ **accessible** [BE] behindertengerecht
disconnect (computer) trennen
discount n der Rabatt; die Ermäßigung
dishes (kitchen) das Geschirr
dishwasher der Geschirrspüler
dishwashing liquid das Geschirrspülmittel
display n (device) das Display; ~ **case** die Vitrine
disposable n der Einwegartikel; ~ **razor** der Einweg-Rasierer
dive v tauchen
diving equipment die Tauchausrüstung
divorce v sich scheiden lassen
dizzy adj schwindelig
doctor n der Arzt
doll n die Puppe
dollar (U.S.) der Dollar
domestic inländisch; ~ **flight** der Inlandsflug
door die Tür

dormitory der Schlafsaal
double bed das Doppelbett
downtown n das Stadtzentrum
dozen das Dutzend
drag lift der Schlepplift
dress (clothing) das Kleid; ~ **code** die Kleiderordnung
drink v trinken; ~ n das Getränk; ~ **menu** die Getränkekarte; ~**ing water** das Trinkwasser
drive v fahren
driver's license number die Führerscheinnummer
drop n (medicine) der Tropfen
drowsiness die Schläfrigkeit
dry clean chemisch reinigen; **~er's** die chemische Reinigung
dubbed synchronisiert
during während
duty (tax) der Zoll; **~-free** zollfrei
DVD die DVD

E

ear das Ohr; **~ache** die Ohrenschmerzen
earlier früher
early früh
earring der Ohrring
east n der Osten
easy leicht
eat v essen
economy class die Economy-Class
elbow n der Ellenbogen

electric outlet die Steckdose
elevator der Fahrstuhl
e-mail v eine E-Mail senden; ~ n die E-Mail; ~ **address** die E-Mail-Adresse
emergency der Notfall; ~ **exit** der Notausgang
empty v entleeren
end v beenden; ~ n das Ende
engaged (person) verlobt
English adj englisch; ~ n **(language)** das Englisch
engrave eingravieren
enjoy genießen
enter v **(place)** eintreten
entertainment die Unterhaltung
entrance der Eingang
envelope der Umschlag
epileptic adj epileptisch; ~ n der Epileptiker
equipment die Ausrüstung
escalator die Rolltreppe
e-ticket das E-Ticket
EU resident der EU-Bürger
euro der Euro
evening n der Abend
excess baggage das Übergepäck
exchange v umtauschen; ~ n **(place)** die Wechselstube; ~ **rate** der Wechselkurs
excursion der Ausflug

excuse v entschuldigen
exhausted erschöpft
exit v verlassen; ~ n der Ausgang
expensive teuer
experienced erfahren
expert der Experte
exposure (film) die Belichtung
express adj Express-; ~ **bus** der Expressbus; ~ **train** der Expresszug
extension (phone) die Durchwahl
extra adj zusätzlich; ~ **large** extragroß
extract v **(tooth)** ziehen
eye das Auge
eyebrow wax die Augenbrauenkorrektur

F

face n das Gesicht
facial n die kosmetische Gesichtsbehandlung
family n die Familie
fan n **(appliance)** der Ventilator
far (distance) weit
farm der Bauernhof
far-sighted weitsichtig
fast adj schnell
fat free fettfrei
father der Vater
fax v faxen; ~ n das Fax; ~ **number** die Faxnummer
fee n die Gebühr
feed v füttern
ferry n die Fähre
fever n das Fieber
field (sports) der Platz
fill v **(car)** tanken

fill out v (form) ausfüllen
filling n (tooth) die Füllung
film n (camera) der Film
fine n (fee for breaking law) die Strafe
finger n der Finger; **~nail** der Fingernagel
fire n das Feuer; **~ department** die Feuerwehr; **~ door** die Feuertür
first adj erste; **~ class** erste Klasse
fit n (clothing) die Passform
fitting room die Umkleidekabine
fix v (repair) reparieren
fixed-price menu das Festpreismenü
flash photography das Fotografieren mit Blitzlicht
flashlight das Blitzlicht
flight n der Flug
flip-flops die Badelatschen
floor n (level) die Etage
florist der Florist
flower n die Blume
folk music die Volksmusik
food das Essen; **~ processor** die Küchenmaschine
foot n der Fuß
football game [BE] das Fußballspiel
for für
forecast n die Vorhersage

forest n der Wald
fork n die Gabel
form n (document) das Formular
formula n (baby) die Babynahrung
fort die Festung
fountain n der Springbrunnen
free adj frei
freelance work die freiberufliche Arbeit
freezer der Gefrierschrank
fresh frisch
friend der Freund
frozen food die Tiefkühlkost
frying pan die Bratpfanne
full-time adj Vollzeit-

G

game n das Spiel
garage n (parking) die Garage; **~** n (for repairs) die Autowerkstatt
garbage bag der Abfallbeutel
gas (car) das Benzin; **~ station** die Tankstelle
gate (airport) das Gate
gay adj (homosexual) schwul; **~ bar** die Schwulenbar; **~ club** der Schwulenclub
gel n (hair) das Gel
generic drug das Generikum
German adj deutsch; **~** n (language) das Deutsch
Germany Deutschland

get off (a train/bus/subway) aussteigen
gift n das Geschenk; **~ shop** der Geschenkwarenladen
girl das Mädchen; **~friend** die Freundin
give v geben
glass (drinking) das Glas; **~ (material)** das Glas
glasses die Brille
go v (somewhere) gehen
gold n das Gold
golf n das Golf; **~ course** der Golfplatz; **~ tournament** das Golfturnier
good adj gut; **~** n die Ware; **~ afternoon** guten Tag; **~ day** guten Tag; **~ evening** guten Abend; **~ morning** guten Morgen; **~bye** auf Wiedersehen
gram das Gramm
grandchild das Enkelkind
grandparents die Großeltern
gray adj grau
green adj grün
grocery store das Lebensmittelgeschäft
ground floor das Erdgeschoss
groundcloth die Unterlegplane
group n die Gruppe
guide n (book) der Reiseführer; **~** n (person) der Fremdenführer **~ dog** der Blindenhund

gym n (place) der Fitnessraum
gynecologist der Gynäkologe

H

hair das Haar; **~brush** die Haarbürste; **~cut** der Haarschnitt; **~ dryer** der Fön; **~ salon** der Friseursalon; **~spray** das Haarspray; **~style** die Frisur; **~ stylist** der Friseur
halal halal
half adj halb; **~** n die Hälfte; **~ hour** die halbe Stunde; **~-kilo** das halbe Kilo
hammer n der Hammer
hand n die Hand; **~ luggage** das Handgepäck; **~ wash** die Handwäsche; **~bag** [BE] die Handtasche
handicapped behindert; **~-accessible** behindertengerecht
hangover der Kater
happy glücklich
hat der Hut
have v haben; **~ sex** Sex haben
hay fever der Heuschnupfen
head (body part) n der Kopf; **~ache** die Kopfschmerzen; **~phones** die Kopfhörer
health die Gesundheit; **~ food store** das Reformhaus
hearing impaired hörgeschädigt

heart das Herz; **~ condition** die Herzkrankheit
heat v heizen; **~er** das Heizgerät; **~ing [BE]** die Heizung
hectare der Hektar
hello Hallo
helmet der Helm
help v helfen; **~** n die Hilfe
here hier
hi Hallo
high hoch; **~chair** der Kindersitz; **~lights (hair)** der Strähnchen; **~way** die Autobahn
hiking boots die Wanderschuhe
hill n der Berg
hire v **[BE] (a car)** mieten; **~ car [BE]** das Mietauto
hockey das Hockey
holiday [BE] der Urlaub
horsetrack die Pferderennbahn
hospital das Krankenhaus
hostel die Jugendherberge
hot (spicy) scharf; **~ (temperature)** heiß; **~ spring** heiße Quelle; **~ water** heißes Wasser
hotel das Hotel
hour die Stunde
house n das Haus; **~hold goods** die Haushaltswaren; **~keeping services** der Hotelservice
how wie; **~ much** wie viel
hug v umarmen
hungry hungrig
hurt v wehtun
husband der Ehemann

I

ibuprofen das Ibuprofen
ice n das Eis; **~ hockey** das Eishockey
icy eisig
identification die Identifikation
ill krank
in in
include v beinhalten
indoor pool (public) das Hallenbad
inexpensive preisgünstig
infected infiziert
information (phone) die Auskunft; **~ desk** die Information
insect das Insekt; **~ bite** der Insektenstich; **~ repellent** der Insektenschutz
insert v **(card)** einführen
insomnia die Schlaflosigkeit
instant message die instant Message
insulin das Insulin
insurance die Versicherung; **~ card** die Versicherungskarte; **~ company** die Versicherungsgesellschaft
interesting interessant
intermediate fortgeschritten
international international; **~ flight** der internationale Flug; **~ student card** der internationale Studentenausweis
internet das Internet; **~ cafe** das Internetcafé; **~ service** der Internetservice
interpreter der Dolmetscher
intersection die Kreuzung
intestine der Darm
introduce v **(person)** vorstellen
invoice n **[BE]** die Rechnung
Ireland das Irland
Irish adj irisch
iron v bügeln; **~** n **(clothes)** das Bügeleisen
Italian adj italienisch

J

jacket n die Jacke
Japanese adj japanisch
jar n **(for jam etc.)** das Glas
jaw der Kiefer
jazz n der Jazz; **~ club** der Jazzclub
jeans die Jeans
jet ski die Jet-Ski
jeweler der Juwelier
jewelry der Schmuck
join v **(go with somebody)** mitkommen
joint n **(body part)** das Gelenk

K

key n der Schlüssel; **~ card** die Schlüsselkarte; **~ring** der Schlüsselring

kiddie pool das Kinderbecken
kidney (body part) die Niere
kilo das Kilo; **~gram** das Kilogramm; **~meter** der Kilometer
kiss v küssen
kitchen die Küche; **~ foil [BE]** die Aluminiumfolie
knee das Knie
knife das Messer
kosher adj koscher

L

lace n **(fabric)** die Spitze
lactose intolerant laktoseintolerant
lake der See
large groß
last adj letzte
late (time) spät
launderette [BE] der Waschsalon
laundromat der Waschsalon
laundry (place) die Wäscherei; **~ service** der Wäscheservice
lawyer n der Anwalt
leather n das Leder
leave v **(hotel)** abreisen; **~ (plane)** abfliegen
left adj, adv **(direction)** links
leg n das Bein
lens die Linse
less weniger
lesson n die Lektion; **take ~s** Unterricht nehmen
letter n der Brief

library die Bücherei
life jacket die Schwimmweste
lifeguard der Rettungsschwimmer
lift n [BE] der Fahrstuhl; ~ n (ride) die Mitfahrgelegenheit; ~ **pass** der Liftpass
light n (cigarette) das Feuer; ~ n (overhead) die Lampe; ~**bulb** die Glühbirne
lighter n das Feuerzeug
like v mögen
line n (train/bus) die Linie
linen das Leinen
lip n die Lippe
liquor store das Spirituosengeschäft
liter der Liter
little wenig
live v leben; ~ **music** Livemusik
liver (body part) die Leber
loafers die Halbschuhe
local n (person) der Einheimische
lock v abschließen; ~ n das Schloss
locker das Schließfach
log off v (computer) abmelden
log on v (computer) anmelden
long adj lang; ~**-sighted** [BE] weitsichtig; ~**-sleeved** langärmlig
look v schauen; ~ **for something** etwas suchen

loose (fit) locker
lose v (something) verlieren
lost verloren; ~**-and-found** das Fundbüro
lotion die Lotion
louder lauter
love v (someone) lieben; ~ n die Liebe
low adj niedrig
luggage das Gepäck; ~ **cart** der Gepäckwagen; ~ **locker** das Gepäckschließfach; ~ **ticket** der Gepäckschein
lunch das Mittagessen
lung die Lunge
luxury car das Luxusauto

M

machine washable maschinenwaschbar
magazine das Magazin
magnificent großartig
mail v mit der Post schicken; ~ n die Post; ~**box** der Briefkasten
main attraction die Hauptattraktion
main course das Hauptgericht
mall das Einkaufszentrum
man (adult male) der Mann
manager der Manager
manicure n die Maniküre
manual car das Auto mit Gangschaltung
map n die Karte; ~ n (town) der Stadtplan

market n der Markt
married verheiratet
marry heiraten
mass n (church service) die Messe
massage n die Massage
match n das Spiel
meal die Mahlzeit
measure v (someone) Maß nehmen
measuring cup der Messbecher
measuring spoon der Messlöffel
mechanic n der Mechaniker
medication (drugs) die Medikamente
medicine die Medikament
medium (steak) medium
meet v treffen
meeting n (business) das Meeting; ~ **room** das Konferenzzimmer
membership card der Mitgliedsausweis
memorial (place) das Denkmal
memory card die Speicherkarte
mend v (clothes) ausbessern
menstrual cramps die Menstruationskrämpfe
menu (restaurant) die Speisekarte
message die Nachricht
meter n (parking) die Parkuhr; ~ n (measure) der Meter
microwave n die Mikrowelle
midday [BE] der Mittag

midnight die Mitternacht
mileage die Meilenzahl
mini-bar die Mini-Bar
minute die Minute
missing (not there) weg
mistake n der Fehler
mobile home der Wohnwagen
mobile phone [BE] das Handy
mobility die Mobilität
monastery das Kloster
money das Geld
month der Monat
mop n der Wischmopp
moped das Moped
more mehr
morning n der Morgen
mosque die Moschee
mother n die Mutter
motion sickness die Reisekrankheit
motor n der Motor; ~ **boat** das Motorboot; ~**cycle** das Motorrad; ~**way** [BE] die Autobahn
mountain n der Berg; ~ **bike** das Mountainbike
mousse (hair) der Schaumfestiger
mouth n der Mund
movie der Film; ~ **theater** das Kino
mug v überfallen
multiple-trip ticket der Mehrfachfahrschein
muscle n der Muskel
museum das Museum
music die Musik; ~ **store** das Musikgeschäft

N

nail file die Nagelfeile
nail salon das Nagelstudio
name n der Name
napkin die Serviette
nappy [BE] die Windel
nationality die Nationalität
nature preserve das Naturreservat
nausea die Übelkeit
nauseous übel
near nahe; **~-sighted** kurzsichtig
nearby in der Nähe von
neck n der Nacken
necklace die Kette
need v brauchen
newspaper die Zeitung
newsstand der Zeitungskiosk
next adj nächste
nice schön
night die Nacht; **~club** der Nachtclub
no nein; **~ (not any)** kein
non-alcoholic nichtalkoholisch
non-smoking adj Nichtraucher
noon n der Mittag
north n der Norden
nose die Nase
note n [BE] (money) der Geldschein
nothing nichts
notify v benachrichtigen
novice der Anfänger
now jetzt
number n die Nummer
nurse n die Krankenschwester

O

office das Büro; **~ hours** die Bürozeiten
off-licence [BE] das Spirituosengeschäft
oil n das Öl
OK okay
old adj alt
on the corner an der Ecke
once (one time) einmal
one ein; **(counting)** eins; **~-day (ticket)** Tages-; **~-way ticket (airline)** das einfache Ticket, **(bus/train/subway)** die Einzelfahrkarte; **~-way street** die Einbahnstraße
only nur
open v öffnen; **~** adj offen
opera die Oper; **~ house** das Opernhaus
opposite n das Gegenteil
optician der Optiker
orange adj (color) orange
orchestra das Orchester
order v (restaurant) bestellen
outdoor pool das Freibad
outside prep draußen
over prep (direction) über; **~done** (meat) zu lang gebraten; **~heat** v (car) überhitzen; **~look** n (scenic place) der Aussichtsplatz; **~night** über Nacht; **~-the-counter (medication)** rezeptfrei
oxygen treatment die Sauerstoffbehandlung

P

p.m. nachmittags
pacifier der Schnuller
pack v packen
package n das Paket
pad n [BE] die Monatsbinde
paddling pool [BE] das Kinderbecken
pain der Schmerz
pajamas der Pyjama
palace der Palast
pants die Hose
pantyhose die Strumpfhose
paper n (material) das Papier; **~ towel** das Papierhandtuch
paracetamol [BE] das Paracetamol
park v parken; **~** n der Park; **~ing garage** das Parkhaus; **~ing lot** der Parkplatz; **~ing meter** die Parkuhr
parliament building das Parlamentsgebäude
part (for car) das Teil; **~-time** adj Teilzeit-
pass through v (travel) durchreisen
passenger der Passagier
passport der Reisepass; **~ control** die Passkontrolle
password das Passwort
pastry shop die Konditorei
patch v (clothing) ausbessern
path der Pfad
pay v bezahlen; **~phone** das öffentliche Telefon
peak n (of a mountain) der Gipfel
pearl n die Perle
pedestrian n der Fußgänger
pediatrician der Kinderarzt
pedicure n die Pediküre
pen n der Stift
penicillin das Penicillin
penis der Penis
per pro; **~ day** pro Tag; **~ hour** pro Stunde; **~ night** pro Nacht; **~ week** pro Woche
perfume n das Parfüm
period (menstrual) die Periode; **~ (of time)** der Zeitraum
permit v erlauben
petrol [BE] das Benzin; **~ station [BE]** die Tankstelle
pewter das Zinn
pharmacy die Apotheke
phone v anrufen; **~** n das Telefon; **~ call** das Telefonat; **~ card** die Telefonkarte; **~ number** die Telefonnummer
photo das Foto; **~copy** die Fotokopie; **~graphy** die Fotografie
pick up v (person) abholen

DICTIONARY

picnic area der Rastplatz
piece *n* das Stück
Pill (birth control) die Pille
pillow *n* das Kissen
pink *adj* rosa
piste [BE] die Piste; ~ **map** [BE] der Pistenplan
pizzeria die Pizzeria
place *v* (a bet) abgeben
plane *n* das Flugzeug
plastic wrap die Klarsichtfolie
plate *n* der Teller
platform [BE] (train) der Bahnsteig
platinum *n* das Platin
play *v* spielen; ~ *n* (theatre) das Stück; **~ground** der Spielplatz; **~pen** der Laufstall
please *adv* bitte
pleasure *n* die Freude
plunger *n* die Saugglocke
plus size die Übergröße
pocket *n* die Tasche
poison *n* das Gift
poles (skiing) die Stöcke
police die Polizei; ~ **report** der Polizeibericht; ~ **station** das Polizeirevier
pond *n* der Teich
pool *n* der Pool
pop music die Popmusik
portion *n* die Portion
post *n* [BE] die Post; ~ **office** die Post; **~box** [BE] der Briefkasten; **~card** die Postkarte

pot *n* der Topf
pottery die Töpferwaren
pound *n* (weight) das Pfund; ~ **(British sterling)** das Pfund
pregnant schwanger
prescribe (medication) verschreiben
prescription das Rezept
press *v* (clothing) bügeln
price *n* der Preis
print *v* drucken; ~ *n* der Ausdruck
problem das Problem
produce *v* die Erzeugnis; ~ **store** das Lebensmittelgeschäft
prohibit verbieten
pronounce aussprechen
Protestant der Protestant
public *adj* öffentlich
pull *v* ziehen
purple *adj* violett
purse *n* die Handtasche
push *v* drücken; **~chair** [BE] der Kinderwagen

Q

quality *n* die Qualität
question *n* die Frage
quiet *adj* leise

R

racetrack die Rennbahn
racket *n* (sports) der Schläger
railway station [BE] der Bahnhof
rain *n* der Regen; **~coat** die Regenjacke; **~forest** der Regenwald; **~y** regnerisch

rap *n* (music) der Rap
rape *v* vergewaltigen; ~ *n* die Vergewaltigung
rare selten
rash *n* der Ausschlag
ravine die Schlucht
razor blade die Rasierklinge
reach *v* erreichen
ready bereit
real *adj* echt
receipt *n* die Quittung
receive *v* erhalten
reception (hotel) die Rezeption
recharge *v* aufladen
recommend empfehlen
recommendation die Empfehlung
recycling das Recycling
red *adj* rot
refrigerator der Kühlschrank
region die Region
registered mail das Einschreiben
regular *n* (fuel) das Normalbenzin
relationship die Beziehung
rent *v* mieten; ~ *n* die Miete
rental car das Mietauto
repair *v* reparieren
repeat *v* wiederholen
reservation die Reservierung; ~ **desk** der Reservierungsschalter
reserve *v* (hotel) reservieren
restaurant das Restaurant
restroom die Toilette

retired *adj* (from work) in Rente
return *v* (something) zurückgeben; ~ *n* [BE] (trip) die Hin- und Rückfahrt
reverse *v* (the charges) [BE] ein R-Gespräch führen
rib *n* (body part) die Rippe
right *adj, adv* (direction) rechts; ~ **of way** die Vorfahrt
ring *n* der Ring
river der Fluss
road map die Straßenkarte
rob *v* berauben
robbed beraubt
romantic *adj* romantisch
room *n* das Zimmer; ~ **key** der Zimmerschlüssel; ~ **service** der Zimmerservice
round trip die Hin- und Rückfahrt
route die Route
rowboat das Ruderboot
rubbing alcohol der Franzbranntwein
rubbish *n* [BE] der Abfall; ~ **bag** [BE] der Abfallbeutel
rugby das Rugby
ruin *n* die Ruine
rush *n* die Eile

S

sad traurig
safe *adj* (protected) sicher; ~ *n* (thing) der Safe
sales tax die Mehrertsteuer

DICTIONARY

same *adj* gleiche
sandals die Sandalen
sanitary napkin die Monatsbinde
sauna die Sauna
sauté *v* sautieren
save *v* **(computer)** speichern
savings (account) das Sparkonto
scanner der Scanner
scarf der Schal
schedule *v* planen; ~ *n* der Plan
school *n* die Schule
science die Wissenschaft
scissors die Schere
sea das Meer
seat *n* der Sitzplatz
security die Sicherheit
see *v* sehen
self-service *n* die Selbstbedienung
sell *v* verkaufen
seminar das Seminar
send *v* senden
senior citizen der Rentner
separated (person) getrennt lebend
serious ernst
service (in a restaurant) die Bedienung
sexually transmitted disease (STD) die sexuell übertragbare Krankheit
shampoo *n* das Shampoo
sharp *adj* scharf
shaving cream die Rasiercreme
sheet *n* **(bed)** die Bettwäsche

ship *v* versenden
shirt das Hemd
shoe store das Schuhgeschäft
shoe der Schuh
shop *v* einkaufen; ~ *n* das Geschäft
shopping *n* das Einkaufen; **~ area** das Einkaufszentrum; **~ centre [BE]** das Einkaufszentrum; **~ mall** das Einkaufszentrum
short kurz; **~-sleeved** kurzärmelig
shorts die kurze Hose
short-sighted [BE] kurzsichtig
shoulder *n* die Schulter
show *v* zeigen
shower *n* **(bath)** die Dusche
shrine der Schrein
sick *adj* krank
side *n* die Seite; **~ dish** die Beilage; **~ effect** die Nebenwirkung; **~ order** die Beilage
sightseeing das Besichtigen von Sehenswürdigkeiten; **~ tour** die Besichtigungstour
sign *v* **(document)** unterschreiben
silk die Seide
silver *n* das Silber
single *adj* **(person)** alleinstehend; **~ bed** das Einzelbett; **~ print** der Einzelabzug; **~ room** das Einzelzimmer
sink *n* das Waschbecken

sister die Schwester
sit *v* sitzen
size *n* die Größe
ski *v* Ski fahren; **~** *n* der Ski; **~ lift** der Skilift
skin *n* die Haut
skirt *n* der Rock
sleep *v* schlafen; **~er car** der Schlafwagen; **~ing bag** der Schlafsack; **~ing car [BE]** der Schlafwagen
slice *n* die Scheibe
slippers die Pantoffeln
slower langsamer
slowly langsam
small klein
smoke *v* rauchen
smoking (area) Raucher-
snack bar der Imbiss
sneakers die Turnschuhe
snowboard *n* das Snowboard
snowshoe *n* der Schneeschuh
snowy verschneit
soap *n* die Seife
soccer der Fußball
sock die Socke
some (with singular nouns) etwas; **~ (with plural nouns)** einige
soother [BE] der Schnuller
sore throat die Halsschmerzen
south *n* der Süden
souvenir *n* das Souvenir; **~ store** das Souvenirgeschäft
spa das Wellness-Center
spatula der Spatel

speak *v* sprechen
specialist (doctor) der Spezialist
specimen die Probe
speeding die Geschwindigkeitsüberschreitung
spell *v* buchstabieren
spicy scharf; **~ (not bland)** würzig
spine (body part) die Wirbelsäule
spoon *n* der Löffel
sports der Sport; **~ massage** die Sportmassage
sprain *n* die Verstauchung
stadium das Stadion
stairs die Treppe
stamp *v* **(ticket)** entwerten; **~** *n* **(postage)** die Briefmarke
start *v* beginnen
starter [BE] die Vorspeise
station *n* **(stop)** die Haltestelle; **bus ~** der Busbahnhof; **gas ~** die Tankstelle; **petrol ~ [BE]** die Tankstelle; **subway ~** die U-Bahn-Haltestelle; **train ~** der Bahnhof
statue die Statue
steakhouse das Steakhouse
steal *v* stehlen
steep *adj* steil
sterling silver das Sterlingsilber
sting *v* der Stich
stolen gestohlen
stomach der Magen; **~ache** die Bauchschmerzen

stool (bowel movement) der Stuhlgang
stop v **(bus)** anhalten; ~ n **(transportation)** die Haltestelle
store directory (mall) der Übersichtsplan
storey [BE] die Etage
stove n der Herd
straight adv **(direction)** geradeaus
strange seltsam
stream n der Strom
stroller (baby) der Kinderwagen
student (university) der Student; ~ **(school)** der Schüler
study v studieren; ~ing n das Studieren
stuffed gefüllt
stunning umwerfend
subtitle n der Untertitel
subway die U-Bahn; ~ **station** die U-Bahn Haltestelle
suit n der Anzug; ~case der Koffer
sun n die Sonne; ~block das Sonnenschutzmittel; ~burn der Sonnenbrand; ~glasses die Sonnenbrille; ~ny sonnig; ~screen die Sonnencreme; ~stroke der Sonnenstich
super n **(fuel)** das Superbenzin; ~market der Supermarkt
surfboard das Surfboard
surgical spirit [BE] der Franzbranntwein

swallow v schlucken
sweater der Pullover
sweatshirt das Sweatshirt
sweet n **[BE]** die Süßigkeit; ~ adj **(taste)** süß
swelling die Schwellung
swim v schwimmen; ~suit der Badeanzug
symbol (keyboard) das Zeichen
synagogue die Synagoge

T
table n der Tisch
tablet (medicine) die Tablette
take v nehmen
tampon n der Tampon
taste v **(test)** kosten
taxi n das Taxi
team n das Team
teaspoon der Teelöffel
telephone n das Telefon
temple (religious) der Tempel
temporary vorübergehend
tennis das Tennis
tent n das Zelt; ~ **peg** der Zelthering; ~ **pole** die Zeltstange
terminal n **(airport)** der Terminal
terrible schrecklich
text v **(send a message)** eine SMS schicken; ~ n der Text
thank v danken; ~ **you** vielen Dank
the der?, das (neuter), die/

theater das Theater
theft der Diebstahl
there dort
thief der Dieb
thigh der Oberschenkel
thirsty durstig
this dieser?, dieses (neuter), diese/
throat der Hals
thunderstorm das Gewitter
ticket n die Fahrkarte; ~ **office** der Fahrkartenschalter
tie n **(clothing)** die Krawatte
tight (fit) eng
tights [BE] die Strumpfhose
time die Zeit; ~table **[BE] (transportation)** der Fahrplan
tire n der Reifen
tired müde
tissue das Gewebe
tobacconist der Tabakhändler
today adv heute
toe n der Zeh
toenail der Zehnagel
toilet [BE] die Toilette; ~ **paper** das Toilettenpapier
tomorrow adv morgen
tongue n die Zunge
tonight heute Abend
to (direction) zu
tooth der Zahn
toothpaste die Zahnpasta
total n **(amount)** der Gesamtbetrag
tough adj **(food)** zäh
tour n die Tour

tourist der Tourist; ~ **information office** das Touristeninformationsbüro
tow truck der Abschleppwagen
towel n das Handtuch
tower n der Turm
town die Stadt; ~ **hall** das Rathaus; ~ **map** der Stadtplan; ~ **square** der Rathausplatz
toy das Spielzeug; ~ **store** der Spielzeugladen
track n **(train)** der Bahnsteig
traditional traditionell
traffic light die Ampel
trail n **(ski)** die Piste; ~ **map** der Pistenplan
trailer (car) der Anhänger
train n der Zug; ~ **station** der Bahnhof
transfer v **(change trains/flights)** umsteigen; ~ **(money)** überweisen
translate übersetzen
trash n der Abfall
travel n das Reisen; ~ **agency** das Reisebüro; ~ **sickness** die Reisekrankheit; ~ers **check [cheque BE]** der Reisescheck
tree der Baum
trim (hair) v nachschneiden
trip n die Reise
trolley [BE] (grocery store) der Einkaufswagen;

~ [BE] (luggage) der Gepäckwagen
trousers [BE] die Hose
T-shirt das T-Shirt
tumble dry maschinentrocknen
turn off v **(device)** ausschalten
turn on v **(device)** anschalten
TV der Fernseher
tyre [BE] der Reifen

U

ugly hässlich
umbrella der Regenschirm
unbranded medication [BE] das Generikum
unconscious (faint) bewusstlos
underdone halb gar
underground n **[BE]** die U-Bahn; **~ station [BE]** die U-Bahn-Haltestelle
underpants [BE] der Slip
understand v verstehen
underwear die Unterwäsche
United Kingdom (U.K.) das Großbritannien
United States (U.S.) die Vereinigten Staaten
university die Universität
unleaded (gas) bleifrei
upset stomach die Magenverstimmung
urgent dringend
urine der Urin
use v benutzen
username der Benutzername
utensil das Haushaltsgerät

V

vacancy (room) das freie Zimmer
vacation der Urlaub
vaccination die Impfung
vacuum cleaner der Staubsauger
vaginal infection die vaginale Entzündung
valid gültig
valley das Tal
valuable adj wertvoll
value n der Wert
van der Kleintransporter
VAT [BE] die Mehrwertsteuer
vegan n der Veganer; **~** adj vegan
vegetarian n der Vegetarier; **~** adj vegetarisch
vehicle registration die Fahrzeugregistrierung
viewpoint (scenic) [BE] der Aussichtsplatz
village das Dorf
vineyard das Weingut
visa das Visum
visit v besuchen; **~ing hours** die Besuchszeiten
visually impaired sehbehindert
vitamin das Vitamin
V-neck der V-Ausschnitt
volleyball game das Volleyballspiel
vomit v erbrechen; **~ing** das Erbrechen

W

wait v warten; **~** n die Wartezeit
waiter der Kellner
waiting room der Warteraum
waitress die Kellnerin
wake v wecken; **~-up call** der Weckruf
walk v spazieren gehen; **~** n der Spaziergang; **~ing route** die Wanderroute
wallet die Geldbörse
war memorial das Kriegsdenkmal
warm (something) erwärmen; **~** adj **(temperature)** warm
washing machine die Waschmaschine
watch v beobachten
waterfall der Wasserfall
wax (hair) mit Wachs entfernen (Haare)
weather n das Wetter
week die Woche; **~end** das Wochenende
weekly wöchentlich
welcome adj willkommen; **you're ~** gern geschehen
west n der Westen
what was
wheelchair der Rollstuhl; **~ ramp** die Rollstuhlrampe
when adv **(at what time)** wann
where wo
white adj weiß; **~ gold** das Weißgold
who (question) wer
widowed verwitwet
wife die Ehefrau
window das Fenster; **~ case** das Schaufenster
wine list die Weinkarte
wireless wireless; **~ phone** das schnurlose Telefon
with mit
withdraw v **(money)** abheben; **~al (bank)** die Abhebung
without ohne
woman die Frau
wool die Wolle
work v arbeiten
wrap v einpacken
wrist das Handgelenk
write v schreiben

Y

year das Jahr
yellow adj gelb
yes ja
yesterday adv gestern
young adj jung
youth hostel die Jugendherberge

Z

zoo der Zoo

DICTIONARY

GERMAN-ENGLISH

A

der Abend evening
das Abendessen dinner
der Abfall n trash [rubbish BE]
der Abfallbeutel garbage [rubbish BE] bag
abfliegen v leave (plane)
der Abflug departure (plane)
abgeben v place (a bet)
abheben v withdraw (money)
die Abhebung withdrawal (bank)
abholen v pick up (something)
ablehnen v decline (credit card)
abmelden v log off (computer)
der Abschleppwagen tow truck
abschließen v lock (door)
der Adapter adapter
die Adresse n address
das Aftershave aftershave
die Agentur agency
AIDS AIDS
die Akupunktur n acupuncture
akzeptieren v accept
allein alone; **~stehend** single (person)
allergisch allergic;
die allergische Reaktion allergic reaction

alt adj old
das Alter n age
die Alternativroute alternate route
die Aluminiumfolie aluminum [kitchen BE] foil
amerikanisch American
die Ampel traffic light
anämisch anemic
die Anästhesie anesthesia
der Anfänger beginner/novice
angreifen v attack
anhalten v stop
der Anhänger trailer
ankommen arrive
die Ankunft arrival
anmelden v log on (computer)
der Anruf n call
anrufen v call
anschalten v turn on (device)
ansteckend contagious
das Antibiotikum n antibiotic
das Antiquitätengeschäft antiques store
antiseptisch antiseptic
der Anwalt lawyer
die Anzahlung n deposit (car rental)
der Anzug n suit
das Apartment apartment
die Apotheke pharmacy [chemist BE]
arbeiten v work

arbeitslos adj unemployed
der Arm n arm (body part)
die Aromatherapie aromatherapy
die Arterie artery
die Arthritis arthritis
der Arzt doctor
asiatisch Asian
das Aspirin aspirin
asthmatisch asthmatic
atmen breathe (place)
attraktiv attractive
auf Wiedersehen goodbye
aufladen v recharge
das Auge eye
ausbessern v mend (clothing)
der Ausfluss discharge (bodily fluid)
ausfüllen v fill out (form)
der Ausgang n exit
ausgeschlafen well-rested
die Auskunft information (phone)
die Ausrüstung equipment
ausschalten turn off (device)
der Ausschlag rash
der Aussichtsplatz viewpoint [BE]
aussprechen pronounce
aussteigen get off (a train/bus/subway)
Australien Australia

der Australier Australian
das Auto car; **~ mit Automatikschaltung** automatic car; **~ mit Gangschaltung** manual car
die Autobahn highway [motorway BE]
automatisch automatic
der Autositz car seat
die Autovermietung car rental [hire BE]

B

das Baby baby
die Babyflasche baby bottle
die Babynahrung formula (baby)
das Baby-Pflegetuch baby wipe
der Babysitter babysitter
backen v bake
die Bäckerei bakery
das Bad bathroom
der Badeanzug swimsuit
die Badelatschen flip-flops
der Bahnhof train [railway BE] station
der Bahnsteig track [platform BE]
das Ballett ballet
die Bank bank (money)
der Bankautomat ATM
die Bankkarte ATM card
die Bar bar (place)

DICTIONARY

das Bargeld *n* cash
der Baseball baseball (game)
der Basketball basketball (game)
die Batterie battery
die Bauchschmerzen stomachache
der Bauernhof *n* farm
der Baum tree
die Baumwolle cotton
die Beaufsichtigung supervision
die Bedienung service (in a restaurant)
beenden *v* exit (computer)
beginnen begin
behindert handicapped; **~engerecht** handicapped (disabled BE)-accessible
beige *adj* beige
die Beilage side order
das Bein leg
beinhalten include (tax)
die Bekleidung clothing
das Bekleidungsgeschäft clothing store
belasten *v* charge (credit card)
belästigen bother
die Belichtung exposure (film)
benachrichtigen notify
benutzen *v* use
der Benutzername username
das Benzin gas [petrol BE]
beobachten *v* watch
der Berater consultant
berauben rob

beraubt robbed
bereit ready
der Berg hill; **~** mountain
beschädigen *v* damage
beschädigt damaged
die Beschwerde complaint
die Beschwerden condition (medical)
der Besen broom
die Besichtigungstour sightseeing tour
besser better
bestätigen confirm
beste *adj* best
bestellen *v* order (restaurant)
besuchen *v* visit
die Besuchszeiten visiting hours
das Bett *n* bed
die Bettwäsche sheets
bewusstlos unconscious (condition)
bezahlen pay
die Beziehung relationship
der BH bra
der Bikini bikini
billig cheap
billiger cheaper
bitte please
die Blase bladder
blau *adj* blue
bleifrei unleaded (gas)
der Blinddarm appendix (body part)
der Blindenhund guide dog
das Blitzlicht flashlight
die Blume *n* flower
die Bluse blouse
das Blut blood

der Blutdruck blood pressure
bluten bleed
der Blutstau congestion
das Boot boat
die Bordkarte boarding pass
der botanische Garten botanical garden
der Boxkampf boxing match
die Bratpfanne frying pan
brauchen *v* need
braun *adj* brown
brechen *v* break
die Bremse brakes (car)
brennen *v* burn
der Brief letter
der Briefkasten mailbox [postbox BE]
die Briefmarke *n* stamp (postage)
die Brille glasses (optical)
bringen bring
britisch British
die Brosche brooch
die Brücke bridge
der Bruder brother
die Brust breast; **~schmerzen** chest pain
das Buch *n* book
die Bücherei library
der Buchladen bookstore
buchstabieren *v* spell
das Bügeleisen *n* iron (clothes)
bügeln *v* iron
das Büro office
die Bürozeiten office hours

der Bus bus; **~bahnhof** bus station; **~fahrschein** bus ticket
die Bushaltestelle bus stop
die Business-Class business class
die Bustour bus tour

C

das Café cafe (place)
campen *v* camp
der Campingkocher camping stove
der Campingplatz campsite
die Campingtoilette chemical toilet
der Canyon canyon
das Casino casino
die CD CD
Celsius Celsius
das Check-in check-in
das Check-out check-out
chinesisch Chinese
der Club *n* club
der Computer computer
die Creme *n* cream (ointment)

D

danken thank
der Darm intestine
das (neuter) the
das Datum *n* date (calendar)
die Decke blanket
das Denkmal memorial (place)
das Deodorant deodorant
der the
das Deutsch German; **~land** Germany

DICTIONARY

der Diabetiker n diabetic
der Diamant diamond
die the
der Dieb thief; **~stahl** theft
diese this
der Diesel diesel
dieser this
dieses (neuter) this
digital digital
der Digitaldruck digital print
das Digitalfoto digital photo
die Digitalkamera digital camera
das Display n display
Dollar dollar (U.S.)
der Dolmetscher interpreter
das Doppelbett double bed
das Dorf village
dort there
der Dosenöffner can opener
draußen outside
dringend urgent
drucken v print
drücken v push
dunkel adj dark
der Durchfall diarrhea
durchreisen pass through
durstig thirsty
die Dusche n shower
das Dutzend dozen
die DVD DVD

E

echt real
die EC-Karte debit card
die Ecke n corner; **an der Ecke** on the corner
die Economy-Class economy class
die Ehefrau wife
der Ehemann husband
die Eile n rush
die Einbahnstraße one-way street
einbrechen v break in (burglary)
einchecken v check in
einführen v insert
der Eingang entrance
eingravieren engrave
der Einheimische n local (person)
einkaufen v shop
das Einkaufen shopping
der Einkaufskorb basket (grocery store)
der Einkaufswagen cart [trolley BE] (grocery store)
das Einkaufszentrum shopping mall [centre BE]; **~** shopping area (town)
einlösen v cash (check)
einmal once
einpacken v wrap (parcel)
eins one
das Einschreiben registered mail
einsteigen v board (bus)
eintreten v enter
der Eintritt admission (fee)
der Einwegartikel n disposable
der Einweg-Rasierer disposable razor

einzahlen v deposit (money)
die Einzahlung n deposit (bank)
der Einzelabzug single print
das Einzelbett single bed
das Einzelzimmer single room
das Eis n ice; **~hockey** ice hockey
der Ellenbogen elbow
die E-Mail n e-mail; **~-Adresse** e-mail address; **~ senden** v e-mail
empfehlen recommend
die Empfehlung recommendation
eng tight (fit)
englisch English
der Enkel grandchild
entleeren v empty
entschuldigen v excuse
entwerten v stamp (ticket)
entwickeln v develop (film)
epileptisch adj epileptic
erbrechen v vomit
erfahren adj experienced
erhalten receive
die Erkältung n cold (sickness)
erklären explain
erlauben allow
ernst serious
erreichen v reach
erschöpft exhausted
erstaunlich amazing
erste Klasse first class
erste adj first

erwärmen v warm (something)
essen eat
das Essen food
das Esszimmer dining room
die Etage floor [storey BE]
das E-Ticket e-ticket
etwas something; **~ mehr...** some more...
der EU-Bürger EU resident
der Euro euro
die Exkursion excursion
der Experte n expert
der Express n express; **~bus** express bus
extra extra; **~ groß** extra large

F

die Fähre ferry
fahren v drive
die Fahrkarte ticket
der Fahrkartenschalter ticket office
das Fahrrad n bicycle
der Fahrradweg bike route
der Fahrstuhl elevator [lift BE]
die Fahrzeugregistrierung vehicle registration
die Familie family
die Farbe n color
das Fax n fax
faxen v fax
die Faxnummer fax number
der Fehler n mistake
fehlen be missing

DICTIONARY

der Urlaub vacation [holiday BE]
das Feinkostgeschäft delicatessen
das Fenster window
der Fernseher television
das Festpreismenü fixed-price menu
die Festung fort
fettfrei fat free
das Feuer fire
die Feuertür fire door
die Feuerwehr fire department
das Feuerzeug lighter
das Fieber fever
filetiert fileted (food)
der Film film (camera); ~ movie (cinema)
der Finger *n* finger
der Fingernagel fingernail
der Fitnessraum gym (workout)
die Flasche bottle
der Flaschenöffner bottle opener
der Fleischer butcher
der Florist florist
der Flug flight
die Fluggesellschaft airline
der Flughafen airport
das Flugzeug airplane
der Fluss river
der Fön hair dryer
das Förderband conveyor belt
das Formular *n* form
fortgeschritten intermediate
das Foto photo
die Fotografie photography

fotografieren take a photo
die Fotokopie photocopy
die Frage *n* question
der Franzbranntwein rubbing alcohol [surgical spirit BE]
die Frau woman
freiberufliche Arbeit freelance work
frei *adj* free
das Fremdenverkehrsbüro tourist information office
die Freude pleasure
der Freund boyfriend; friend
die Freundin girlfriend; friend
frisch fresh
die Frischhaltefolie plastic wrap
der Friseur barber, hairstylist
der Friseursalon hair salon
die Frisur hairstyle
früh early
das Frühstück breakfast
der Führer guide
die Führerscheinnummer driver's license number
das Fundbüro lost-and-found
für for
der Fuß foot; ~ball soccer
das Fußballspiel soccer match [football game BE]
der Fußgänger *n* pedestrian

das Fußgelenk *n* ankle
füttern *v* feed

G

die Gabel fork
der Gang aisle
die Garage garage
das Gate gate (airport)
das Gebäude building
geben *v* give
die Gebühr fee
der Geburtstag birthday
gefährlich dangerous
der Gefrierschrank freezer
das Gegenteil *n* opposite
gehen *v* go (somewhere)
gekocht stewed
das Gel gel (hair)
gelb *adj* yellow
das Gelbgold yellow gold
das Geld money
die Geldbörse wallet
der Geldschein *n* bill [note BE] (money)
das Gelenk joint (body part)
das Generikum generic drug [unbranded medication BE]
genießen *v* enjoy
das Gepäck baggage [luggage BE]
die Gepäckausgabe baggage claim
der Gepäckschein baggage [luggage BE] ticket
das Gepäckschließfach baggage [luggage BE] locker

der Gepäckwagen baggage [luggage BE] cart
geradeaus straight
gern geschehen you're welcome
das Geschäft business; ~ store ~sverzeichnis store directory; ~szentrum business center
das Geschenk gift
der Geschenkwarenladen gift shop
das Geschirr dishes (kitchen)
der Geschirrspüler dishwasher
das Geschirrspülmittel dishwashing liquid
geschlossen closed
die Geschwindigkeitsüberschreitung speeding
das Gesicht *n* face
gestern yesterday
gestohlen stolen
die Gesundheit health
das Getränk *n* drink
die Getränkekarte drink menu
getrennt lebend separated (person)
das Gewitter thunderstorm
gewürfelt diced (food)
das Gift *n* poison
der Gipfel peak (of a mountain)
das Girokonto checking [current BE] account
das Glas glass
gleich same
glücklich happy

155

DICTIONARY

die Glühbirne lightbulb
golden golden
der Golfplatz golf course
das Golfturnier golf tournament
das Grad degree (temperature)
das Gramm gram
grau *adj* gray
der Grill *n* barbecue
groß big; **~ large**
großartig magnificent
das Großbritannien United Kingdom (U.K.)
die Größe *n* size
die Großeltern grandparents
größer bigger; **~ larger**
grün *adj* green
die Gruppe *n* group
gültig valid
der Gürtel belt
gut *adj* good; *adv* well; **~enAbend** good evening; **~en Morgen** good morning; **~en Tag** good day
der Gynäkologe gynecologist

H

das Haar hair
die Haarbürste hairbrush
der Harfestiger mousse (hair)
der Haarschnitt haircut
das Haarspray hairspray
haben *v* have
halal halal
halb half; **~gar** underdone; **die ~e Stunde** half hour; **das ~e Kilo** half-kilo

die Halbschuhe loafers
halbtags part-time
das Hallenbad indoor pool
Hallo hello
der Hals throat
die Halsschmerzen sore throat
die Haltestelle *n* stop
der Hammer hammer
die Hand *n* hand
das Handgelenk wrist
das Handgepäck hand luggage
die Handtasche purse (handbag BE)
das Handtuch towel
Handwäsche hand wash
das Handy cell [mobile BE] phone
hässlich ugly
die Hauptattraktion main attraction
das Hauptgericht main course
das Haus *n* house
das Haushaltsgerät utensil
die Haushaltswaren household goods
die Haut *n* skin
heiraten *v* marry
heiß hot (temperature); **~eQuelle** hot spring; **~esWasser** hot water
heizen *v* heat
die Heizung heating
der Hektar hectare
helfen *v* help
der Helm helmet
das Hemd shirt
der Herd stove
das Herz heart

die Herzkrankheit heart condition
der Heuschnupfen hay fever
heute today; **~ Abend** tonight
hier here
die Hilfe *n* help
die Hin- und Rückfahrt round-trip
Hinfahrt- one-way (ticket)
hinter behind (direction)
hoch high
das Hockey hockey
die Höhle *n* cave
hörgeschädigt hearing impaired
die Hose pants [trousers BE]
das Hotel hotel
hungrig hungry
husten *v* cough
der Husten cough
der Hut hat

I

das Ibuprofen ibuprofen
die Identifikation identification
die Impfung vaccination
in in
infiziert infected
die Information information; **~ information desk**
inländisch domestic
der Inlandsflug domestic flight
das Insekt bug
der Insektenschutz insect repellent
der Insektenstich insect bite

die Instant Message instant message
das Insulin insulin
interessant interesting
international international; **der ~e Studentenausweis** international student card; **der ~e Flug** international flight
das Internet internet; **~café** internet cafe
der Internet-Service internet service
irisch *adj* Irish
Irland Ireland
italienisch *adj* Italian

J

ja yes
die Jacke jacket
das Jahr year
japanisch *adj* Japanese
der Jazz jazz; **~club** jazz club
die Jeans jeans
der Jeansstoff denim
der Jet-ski jet ski
jetzt now
die Jugendherberge hostel; **~ youth hostel**
jung *adj* young
der Junge boy
der Juwelier jeweler

K

das Kabarett cabaret
das Kaffeehaus coffee house
die Kalorie calorie
kalt *adj* cold (temperature); **~ cool (temperature)**
die Kamera camera

die Kameratasche camera case
der Kamm n comb
das Kanada Canada
kanadisch adj Canadian
die Karaffe carafe
die Karte n card; ~ map
der Kassierer cashier
der Kater hangover (alcohol)
die Kathedrale cathedral
kaufen v buy
das Kaufhaus department store
der Kaugummi chewing gum
der Kellner waiter
die Kellnerin waitress
die Kette necklace
der Kiefer jaw
das Kilo kilo; ~gramm kilogram
der Kilometer kilometer
das Kind child
der Kinderarzt pediatrician
das Kinderbecken kiddie pool
das Kinderbett cot
die Kinderkarte children's menu
die Kinderportion children's portion
der Kindersitz highchair
der Kinderstuhl child's seat
der Kinderwagen stroller
das Kino movie theater
die Kirche church
das Kissen pillow

die Klarsichtfolie plastic wrap (cling film BE)
die Klasse class
die klassische Musik classical music
das Kleid n dress (clothing)
die Kleiderordnung dress code
klein small
der Kleintransporter van
die Klimaanlage air conditioning
die Klippe cliff
das Kloster monastery
das Knie n knee
der Knochen n bone
kochen v boil; ~ cook
das Kölnischwasser cologne
der Koffer suitcase
der Kollege colleague
kommen v come
die Konditorei pastry shop
das Kondom condom
die Konferenz conference
das Konferenzzimmer meeting room
der Kongressaal convention hall
die Konserve canned good
das Konsulat consulate
kontaktieren v contact
die Kontaktlinse contact lens
die Kontaktlinsenlösung contact lens solution
das Konto n account

das Konzert concert
die Konzerthalle concert hall
der Kopf n head (body part)
die Kopfhörer headphones
die Kopfschmerzen headache
der Korkenzieher corkscrew
koscher kosher
kosmetisch adj cosmetic; ~e Gesichtsbehandlung facial (treatment)
kosten v cost; ~ taste
krank ill; ~ sick
das Krankenhaus hospital
die Krankenschwester n nurse
der Krankenwagen ambulance
die Krawatte tie (clothing)
die Kreditkarte credit card
die Kreuzung intersection
das Kriegsdenkmal war memorial
das Kristall crystal (glass)
die Küche kitchen
die Küchenmaschine food processor
der Kühlschrank refrigerator
die Kunst art
das Kupfer copper
kurz short; ~e Hose shorts
kurzärmelig short-sleeved

kurzsichtig near-[short- BE] sighted
küssen v kiss

L

laktoseintolerant lactose intolerant
die Lampe n light (overhead)
die Landesvorwahl country code
landwirtschaftliches Erzeugnis produce
lang adj long; ~ärmlig long-sleeved;
langsam slow; ~er slower
langweilig boring
der Laufstall playpen
lauter louder
leben v live
das Lebensmittelgeschäft grocery store
die Leber liver (body part)
lecker delicious
das Leder leather
leicht easy
das Leinen linen
leise quiet
die Lektion lesson
letzte adj last
die Liebe n love
lieben v love (someone)
der Liegestuhl deck chair (ferry)
der Liftpass lift pass
die Linie line (train)
links left (direction)
die Linse lens
die Lippe lip
der Liter liter
Livemusik live music
locker loose (fit)
der Löffel n spoon

löschen v clear (on an ATM); ~ v delete (computer)
die Lotion lotion
die Luftpost n airmail
die Luftpumpe air pump
lufttrocknen v air dry
die Lunge lung

M

das Mädchen girl
das Magazin magazine
der Magen stomach
die Magenverstimmung upset stomach
die Mahlzeit meal
der Manager manager
die Maniküre n manicure
der Mann man (male)
der Mantel n coat
der Markt market
maschinentrocknen tumble dry
die Massage n massage
mechanisch adj mechanic
das Medikament medicine
die Medikamente medication
medium adj medium (meat)
das Meer sea
mehr more
die Mehrwertsteuer sales tax [VAT BE]
die Menstruationskrämpfe menstrual cramps
die Messe mass (church service)

messen v measure (someone)
das Messer knife
der Messbecher measuring cup
der Messlöffel measuring spoon
das Mietauto rental [hire BE] car
mieten v rent [hire BE]
die Mikrowelle n microwave
mild mild
die Mini-Bar mini-bar
die Minute minute
mit with; ~ **Bedienung** full-service
die Mitgliedskarte membership card
mitkommen v join
mitnehmen give somebody a lift (ride)
Mittag noon [midday BE]
das Mittagessen n lunch
Mitternacht midnight
der Mixer blender
die Mobilität mobility
mögen v like
der Monat month
die Monatsbinde sanitary napkin [pad BE]
der Mopp n mop
das Moped moped
morgen tomorrow
der Morgen morning
die Moschee mosque
der Moslem Muslim
das Motorboot motor boat
das Motorrad motorcycle
das Mountainbike mountain bike

müde tired
der Mund mouth
die Münze coin
das Münztelefon pay phone
das Museum museum
die Musik music
das Musikgeschäft music store
der Muskel muscle
die Mutter mother

N

nach after
der Nachmittag afternoon
nachprüfen v check (on something)
die Nachricht message
nachschneiden trim (haircut)
nächste adj next
die Nacht night
der Nachtclub nightclub
der Nacken neck
die Nagelfeile nail file
das Nagelstudio nail salon
nahe prep near
die Nähe vicinity; **in der Nähe** nearby
der Name n name
die Nase nose
die Nationalität nationality
das Naturreservat nature preserve
die Nebenstelle extension (phone)
die Nebenwirkung side effect
nehmen v take
nein no

Nichtraucher- non-smoking (area)
nichts nothing
niedrig low
die Niere kidney (body part)
der Norden n north
normal regular
der Notausgang emergency exit
der Notfall emergency
die Nummer n number
nur only; ~ just

O

obere adj upper
der Oberschenkel thigh
offen adj open
öffentlich adj public
öffnen v open
die Öffnungszeiten business hours
ohne without
das Ohr ear
die Ohrenschmerzen earache
der Ohrring earring
OK okay
das Öl n oil
die Oper opera
das Opernhaus opera house
der Optiker optician
orange adj orange (color)
das Orchester orchestra
die Ortsvorwahl area code
der Osten n east

P

packen v pack
die Packung carton; ~ packet

das Paket package
der Palast palace
paniert breaded
die Panne breakdown (car)
die Pantoffeln slippers
das Papier n paper
das Papierhandtuch paper towel
das Paracetamol acetaminophen [paracetamol BE]
das Parfüm n perfume
der Park park
parken v park
das Parkhaus parking garage
der Parkplatz parking lot [car park BE]
die Parkuhr parking meter
das Parlamentsgebäude parliament building
das Parterre ground floor
der Passagier passenger
die Passform fit (clothing)
die Passkontrolle passport control
das Passwort password
die Pediküre pedicure
das Penicillin penicillin
der Penis penis
die Pension bed and breakfast
die Periode period (menstrual)
die Perle pearl
der Pfad path
die Pferderennbahn horsetrack

das Pflaster bandage
das Pfund n pound (weight)
das Pfund pound (British sterling)
die Pille Pill (birth control)
die Piste n trail [piste BE]
der Pistenplan trail [piste BE] map
die Pizzeria pizzeria
der Plan n schedule [timetable BE]; ~ map
planen v plan
das Platin platinum
die Platte flat tire
der Platz field (sports); ~ seat; ~ am Gang aisle seat
die Plombe filling (tooth)
der Po buttocks
die Polizei police
der Polizeibericht police report
das Polizeirevier police station
der Pool n pool
die Popmusik pop music
die Portion n portion
die Post mail [post BE]; ~ post office
die Postkarte postcard
der Preis price; ~ pro Gedeck cover charge
preisgünstig inexpensive
pro per; ~ **Nacht** per night; ~ **Stunde** per hour; ~ **Tag** per day; ~ **Woche** per week
das Problem problem
Prost! Cheers!

die Prothese denture
die Puppe doll
der Pyjama pajamas

Q
die Qualität n quality
die Quittung receipt

R
das R-Gespräch collect call [reverse charge call BE]
ein R-Gespräch führen v call collect [to reverse the charges BE]
der Rabatt discount
das Radfahren cycling
der Rap rap (music)
die Rasiercreme shaving cream
die Rasierklinge razor blade
der Rastplatz picnic area
das Rathaus town hall
der Rathausplatz town square
rauchen v smoke
Raucher- smoking (area)
die Rechnung bill [invoice BE] (of sale)
rechts right (direction)
das Recycling recycling
das Reformhaus health food store
der Regen n rain
die Regenjacke raincoat
der Regenschirm umbrella
der Regenwald rainforest

die Region region
regnerisch rainy
der Reifen tire [tyre BE]
reinigen v clean; **chemisch ~** dry clean
die Reinigung dry cleaner's
die Reinigungsmittel cleaning supplies
die Reise trip; ~ journey
das Reisebüro travel agency
der Reiseführer guide book
die Reisekrankheit motion sickness
der Reisepass passport
der Reisescheck traveler's check [cheque BE]
die Rennbahn racetrack
der Rentner senior citizen
reparieren v fix; ~ repair
reservieren v reserve
die Reservierung reservation
der Reservierungsschalter reservation desk
das Restaurant restaurant
der Rettungsschwimmer lifeguard
das Rezept prescription
die Rezeption reception
die Richtung direction
der Ring n ring
die Rippe rib (body part)

der Rock skirt
der Rollstuhl wheelchair
die Rollstuhlrampe wheelchair ramp
die Rolltreppe escalator
romantisch romantic
rosa *adj* pink
rot *adj* red
die Route route
der Rücken back (body part)
die Rückenschmerzen backache
der Rucksack backpack
das Ruderboot rowboat
das Rugby rugby
die Ruine ruin

S

der Safe *n* safe (for valuables)
die Sandalen sandals
sauber *adj* clean
die Sauerstoffbehandlung oxygen treatment
die Saugglocke plunger
die Sauna sauna
der Scanner scanner
die Schachtel *n* pack; ~ **Zigaretten** pack of cigarettes
der Schal scarf
scharf hot (spicy); ~ sharp
das Schaufenster window case
der Scheck check [cheque BE] (payment)
die Schere scissors
schicken send; **per Post** ~ mail
das Schlachtfeld battleground
schlafen *v* sleep
die Schläfrigkeit drowsiness
der Schlafsack sleeping bag
die Schlafstörung insomnia
der Schlafwagen sleeper [sleeping BE] car
der Schläger racket (sports)
schlecht nauseous; ~ bad
der Schlepplift drag lift
schließen *v* close (a shop)
das Schließfach locker
das Schloss castle; ~ lock
die Schlucht ravine
der Schlüssel key; ~**ring** key ring
die Schlüsselkarte key card
der Schmerz pain; **Schmerzen haben** be in pain
der Schmuck jewelry
schmutzig dirty
der Schneeschuh snowshoe
schneiden *v* cut
schnell fast
der Schnellzug express train
der Schnitt *n* cut (injury)
der Schnuller pacifier [soother BE]

schön nice; ~ beautiful
schrecklich terrible
schreiben write
der Schrein shrine
der Schuh shoe
das Schuhgeschäft shoe store
die Schule school
die Schulter shoulder
die Schüssel bowl
schwanger pregnant
schwarz *adj* black
die Schwellung swelling
die Schwester sister
schwierig difficult
das Schwimmbad swimming pool
schwimmen *v* swim
die Schwimmweste life jacket
schwindelig dizzy
schwul *adj* gay
die Schwulenbar gay bar
der Schwulenclub gay club
der See lake
sehbehindert visually impaired
sehen *v* look; ~ see
die Sehenswürdigkeit attraction
die Seide silk
die Seife *n* soap
die Seilbahn cable car
sein *v* be
die Selbstbedienung self-service
selten rare
seltsam strange
das Seminar seminar
senden *v* send
die Serviette napkin
der Sessellift chair lift

sexuell übertragbare Krankheit sexually transmitted disease (STD)
das Shampoo *n* shampoo
sich scheiden lassen *v* divorce
sicher *adj* safe (protected)
die Sicherheit security
das Sieb colander
das Sightseeing sightseeing
das Silber *n* silver
sitzen *v* sit
der Ski *n* ski
Ski fahren *v* ski
der Skilift ski lift
der Slip briefs (clothing)
die SMS SMS; **eine SMS schicken** *v* text (message)
das Snowboard *n* snowboard
die Socke sock
die Sonne *n* sun
der Sonnenbrand sunburn
die Sonnenbrille sunglasses
die Sonnencreme sunscreen
der Sonnenstich sunstroke
sonnig sunny
das Souvenir souvenir; ~**geschäft** souvenir store
das Sparkonto savings (account)
spät late (time)
der Spatel spatula
später later

spazieren gehen *v* walk
der Spaziergang *n* walk
die Speicherkarte memory card
speichern *v* save (computer)
die Speisekarte menu
der Spezialist specialist (doctor)
das Spiel game; ~ match
spielen *v* play
die Spielhalle arcade
der Spielplatz playground
das Spielzeug toy
der Spielzeugladen toy store
das Spirituosengeschäft liquor store [off-licence BE]
die Spitze lace (fabric)
der Sport sports
die Sportmassage sports massage
das Sportgeschäft sporting goods store
sprechen *v* speak
der Springbrunnen fountain
die Spülung conditioner (hair)
die Stäbchen chopsticks
das Stadion stadium
die Stadt city; ~ town
der Stadtplan town map
die Stadtrundfahrt sightseeing tour
das Stadtzentrum downtown area

die Stange carton (of cigarettes)
die Statue statue
der Staubsauger vacuum cleaner
das Steakhouse steakhouse
die Steckdose electric outlet
stehlen *v* steal
steil steep
das Sterlingsilber sterling silver
der Stich *n* sting
die Stiefel boots
der Stift pen
stillen breastfeed
die Stöcke poles (skiing)
stornieren *v* cancel
die Strafe *n* fine (fee for breaking law)
die Strähnchen highlights (hair)
der Strand beach
die Straßenkarte road map
der Strom electricity
die Strumpfhose pantyhose [tights BE]
das Stück *n* piece; ~ play (theater); ~ slice
der Student student
studieren *v* study
der Stuhl chair
der Stuhlgang stool (bowel movement)
die Stunde hour
der Süden *n* south
das Super super (fuel)
der Supermarkt supermarket
das Surfboard surfboard

das Surfbrett windsurfer (board)
süß cute; ~ sweet (taste)
die Süßigkeit candy [sweet BE]
das Sweatshirt sweatshirt
die Synagoge synagogue
synchronisiert dubbed

T

der Tabakhändler tobacconist
die Tablette tablet (medicine)
der Tag day
Tages- one-day (ticket)
das Tal valley
der Tampon tampon
tanken *v* fill (car)
die Tankstelle gas [petrol BE] station
der Tanzclub dance club
tanzen *v* dance
die Tasche bag; ~ pocket
die Tasse *n* cup
taub *adj* deaf
die Tauchausrüstung diving equipment
tauchen *v* dive
das Taxi taxi
das Team team
der Teelöffel teaspoon
der Teich pond
das Teil (for car)
das Telefon *n* phone
das schnurlose Telefon wireless phone
der Telefonanruf phone call

die Telefonkarte phone card
die Telefonnummer phone number
der Teller plate
der Tempel temple (religious)
das Tennis tennis
der Termin appointment
der Terminal terminal (airport)
teuer expensive
der Text *n* text
das Theater theater
tief deep
die Tiefkühlkost frozen food
das Tier animal
der Tisch table
die Toilette restroom [toilet BE]
das Toilettenpapier toilet paper
der Topf *n* pot
die Töpferwaren pottery (pots)
die Tour *n* tour
der Tourist tourist
traditionell traditional
traurig sad
treffen meet
das Treffen meeting
trennen disconnect (computer)
die Treppe stairs
trinken *v* drink
das Trinkwasser drinking water
der Tropfen *n* drop (medicine)
das T-Shirt T-shirt
die Tür door
der Turm tower

DICTIONARY

die Turnschuhe sneaker

U

die U-Bahn subway [underground BE]
die U-Bahn-Haltestelle subway [underground BE] station
über prep over; **~ Nacht** overnight; **~fallen** v mug
die Übergröße plus size
überhitzen overheat (car)
übersetzen translate
überweisen v transfer (money)
um (die Ecke) around (the corner)
umändern alter
umarmen hug
die Umkleidekabine fitting room
der Umschlag envelope
umsteigen v change (buses); **~** v transfer (change trains/flights)
umtauschen v exchange (money)
umwerfend stunning
unbeaufsichtigt unattended
der Unfall accident
die Universität university
die Unterhaltung entertainment (amusement)
die Unterhose underwear [underpants BE]
die Unterkunft accommodation
die Unterlegplane groundcloth

unterschreiben v sign
der Untertitel n subtitle
die Unterwäsche underwear
der Urin urine
der Urlaub vacation [BE holiday]

V

die Vagina vagina
vaginal vaginal; **die ~e Entzündung** vaginal infection
der Vater father
der V-Ausschnitt V-neck
der Veganer n vegan
der Vegetarier n vegetarian
der Ventilator fan (appliance)
verbieten v prohibit
verbinden v connect (internet)
die Verbindung connection
die Vereinigten Staaten United States (U.S.)
verfügbar available
vergewaltigen v rape
die Vergewaltigung n rape
der Vergnügungspark amusement park
verheiratet married
verkaufen v sell
verlangen v charge (cost)
verlieren v lose (something)
verlobt engaged
verloren lost

verschlucken v swallow
verschneit snowy
verschreiben v prescribe (medication)
versenden v ship
die Versicherung insurance
die Versicherungsgesellschaft insurance company
die Versicherungskarte insurance card
die Verstauchung n sprain
verstehen understand
die Verstopfung constipation
verwitwet widowed
verzögern v delay
viel much; **~ a lot**; **~en Dank** thank you; **wie ~** how much
violett adj purple
die Visitenkarte business card
das Visum visa
das Vitamin vitamin
die Vitrine display case
der Vogel bird
die Volksmusik folk music
das Volleyballspiel volleyball game
Vollzeit- full-time
vor before; **Viertel ~ vier** a quarter to four
die Vorfahrt right of way
die Vorhersage n forecast
die Vorspeise appetizer [starter BE]

vorstellen v introduce (person)
vorübergehend temporary

W

wählen v dial
während during
die Währung currency
der Währungsumtausch currency exchange
der Wald forest
die Wanderroute walking route
die Wanderschuhe hiking boots
die Wanduhr wall clock
wann when (time)
die Ware n good; **~ product**
die Waren goods
warm adj warm (temperature)
warten wait
der Warteraum waiting room
die Wartezeit n waiting period
was what
das Waschbecken n sink
die Wäscherei laundry (facility)
der Wäscheservice laundry service
die Waschmaschine washing machine
waschmaschinenfest machine washable
das Waschmittel detergent
der Waschsalon laundromat [launderette BE]

DICTIONARY

der Wasserfall waterfall
die Wasserski water skis
das Wechselgeld *n* change (money)
der Wechselkurs exchange rate
wechseln *v* change
die Wechselstube currency exchange office
wecken *v* wake
der Weckruf wake-up call
weich soft
das Weingut vineyard
die Weinkarte wine list
weiß *adj* white
das Weißgold white gold
weit *adv* far (distance); ~ *adj* loose (fit)
weitsichtig far [long BE]- sighted
das Wellness-Center spa
wenig *adj* little (not much)
weniger less
wer who
der Wert value
wertvoll valuable
der Westen *n* west
das Wetter weather
wickeln *v* change (baby)
wie how; **~ viel** how much
wiederholen repeat
willkommen *adj* welcome
die Windel diaper [nappy BE]
die Wirbelsäule spine (body part)
wireless wireless
wo where
die Woche week
das Wochenende weekend
wöchentlich weekly
der Wohnwagen mobile home
die Wolle wool
wunder schön beautiful
die Wüste *n* desert

Z

der Zahn tooth
der Zahnarzt dentist
die Zahnpaste toothpaste
der Zeh *n* toe
der Zehennagel toenail
das Zeichen symbol (keyboard)
zeigen *v* show (somebody something)
die Zeit time
der Zeitraum period (of time)
die Zeitung newspaper
der Zeitungskiosk newsstand
das Zelt tent
der Zelthering tent peg
die Zeltstange tent pole
der Zentimeter centimeter
zerbrochen broken (smashed)
das Zertifikat certificate
ziehen *v* extract (tooth); ~ *v* pull (door sign)
die Zigarette cigarette
die Zigarre cigar
das Zimmer room
der Zimmerschlüssel room key
der Zimmerservice room service
das Zinn pewter
der Zoll customs; ~ **duty** (tax)
zollfrei duty-free
der Zoo zoo
zu *adv* too; ~ *prep* to
der Zug train
die Zunge tongue
zurückgeben *v* return (something)
der Zutritt *n* access

INDEX

Alte Pinakothek 54
Alter Hof 37
Altes Rathaus 32
Ammersee 74
Asamhaus 41
Asamkirche 40
Augsburg 84

Bayerisches Eisenbahnmuseum 82
Bayerisches Nationalmuseum 62
Berchtesgaden 76
BMW Museum 70
Brunnenhof 46
Burg Harburg 83

Chiemsee 76
Chinesischer Turm 61

Dachau Concentration Camp Memorial Site 78
DB Museum 87
Deutsches Jagd- und Fischereimuseum 41
Dinkelsbühl 82
Dokumentation Obersalzberg 77
Donauwörth 83
Dreifaltigkeitskirche 42

Eagle's Nest 77
Englischer Garten 60
Ettal 73

Feldherrnhalle 48
Fischbrunnen 32
Flugwerft Schleißheim 79
Frauenchiemsee 76
Frauenkirche 34

Freising 79
Friedensengel 62
Fuggerei 84
Fünf Höfe 47
Fussgängerzone 41

Germanisches Nationalmuseum 87
Glockenspiel 33
Glyptothek 52

Haidhausen 64
Haus der Kunst 61
Heiliggeistkirche 36
Herrenchiemsee 76
Hofbräuhaus 37
Hofgarten 49
Hohenschwangau 72

Isartor 38

Japanese Tea House 61
Jüdisches Museum 40
Jüdisches Zentrum am Jakobsplatz 40
Jugendstil Museum 62

Karlstor 42
Kleinhesseloher See 61
Königsee 78
Königsplatz 49
Kulturzentrum am Gasteig 64

Landsberg am Lech 71
Language 124
Lenbachhaus 53
Leopoldstrasse 59
Leuchtenberg Palais 49
Linderhof 74
Ludwigstrasse 49

Marienaltar 36
Marienplatz 31
Mariensäule 31
Maximilianeum 63
Maximilian Residenz 46
Maximilianstrasse 44, 63
Max-Joseph-Platz 43
Monopteros 61
Müller'sches Volksbad 64
Münchner Stadtmuseum 39
Museum Brandhorst 57
Museum of the Bavarian Kings 73

Nationalparkhaus 77
Nationaltheater 44
Neue Pinakothek 56
Neues Rathaus 33
Neuschwanstein Castle 72
Nördlingen 82
Nuremberg 86

Oberammergau 73
Odeonsplatz 47
Oktoberfest 92
Olympiapark 69

Pinakothek der Moderne 56
Propyläen 50

Residenz 43
Residenzmuseum 44
Residenztheater 44
Richard Strauss-Brunnen 42
Rinderbrunnen 39
Romantic Road 80
Rothenburg ob der Tauber 81

INDEX

Schloss Nymphenburg 66
Schloss Schleißheim 79
Siegestor 58
Spielzeugmuseum 32
Staatliche Antikensammlungen 51
Staatsbrauerei Weihenstephan 80
Städtische Galerie im Lenbachaus 53

Starnberg 75
Starnberger See 75
St Johann Baptist Church 71
St Ludwig's 59
St Michael's 41
St Peter's 35

Theatinerkirche 48
Theatinerstrasse 47

Viktualienmarkt 36
Villa Stuck 62
Völkerkundemuseum 63

Weisses Bräuhaus 38
Wieskirche 71
Wittelsbacher Brunnen 42
Würzburg 80

Youth Hostels 131

Berlitz pocket guide

MUNICH AND BAVARIA

Eighth Edition 2018

Editor: Sian Marsh
Author: Jack Altman
Head of Production: Rebeka Davies
Picture Editor: Tom Smyth
Cartography Update: Carte
Update Production: Apa Digital
Photography Credits: Alamy 95; Apa 40, 46, 48, 52, 67, 68, 74, 93, 96, 99, 102; AWL Images 1; Deutsches Museum 65; Dreamstime 79, 83, 87; Fotolia 105; Getty Images 4MC, 5T, 5M, 18, 26, 30, 57, 58, 63, 88; Glyn Genin/Apa Publications 38, 81, 85 iStock 4TC, 4ML, 5TC, 5MC, 5MC, 6L, 7, 7R, 11, 13, 17, 20, 33, 61, 71, 73, 77, 91; Public domain 5M, 23, 25, 55; Ra Boe/Wikipedia 15; Shutterstock 4TL, 35, 36, 42, 44, 50, 100
Cover Picture: iStock

Distribution
UK, Ireland and Europe: Apa Publications (UK) Ltd; sales@insightguides.com
United States and Canada: Ingram Publisher Services; ips@ingramcontent.com
Australia and New Zealand: Woodslane; info@woodslane.com.au
Southeast Asia: Apa Publications (SN) Pte; singaporeoffice@insightguides.com
Worldwide: Apa Publications (UK) Ltd; sales@insightguides.com

Special Sales, Content Licensing and CoPublishing
Insight Guides can be purchased in bulk quantities at discounted prices. We can create special editions, personalised jackets and corporate imprints tailored to your needs. sales@insightguides.com; www.insightguides.biz

All Rights Reserved
© 2018 Apa Digital (CH) AG and Apa Publications (UK) Ltd

Printed in China by CTPS

No part of this book may be reproduced, stored in a retrieval system or transmitted in any form or means electronic, mechanical, photocopying, recording or otherwise, without prior written permission from Apa Publications.

Contact us
Every effort has been made to provide accurate information in this publication, but changes are inevitable. The publisher cannot be responsible for any resulting loss, inconvenience or injury. We would appreciate it if readers would call our attention to any errors or outdated information. We also welcome your suggestions; please contact us at: berlitz@apaguide.co.uk
www.insightguides.com/berlitz

Berlitz Trademark Reg. U.S. Patent Office and other countries. Marca Registrada. Used under licence from the Berlitz Investment Corporation

Schnel

Berlitz®

speaking your language

phrase book & dictionary
phrase book & CD

Available in: Arabic, Brazilian Portuguese*, Burmese*, Cantonese Chinese, Croatian, Czech*, Danish*, Dutch, English, Filipino, Finnish*, French, German, Greek, Hebrew*, Hindi*, Hungarian*, Indonesian, Italian, Japanese, Korean, Latin American Spanish, Malay, Mandarin Chinese, Mexican Spanish, Norwegian, Polish, Portuguese, Romanian*, Russian, Spanish, Swedish, Thai, Turkish, Vietnamese
*Book only

www.berlitzpublishing.com